Presented to: _____

By: _____

God's
Promises.
for Women

THOMAS NELSON
Since 1798

NASHVILLE DALLAS MEXICO CITY RIO DE JANEIRO BEIJING

ISBN: 08499-5620-X

Contents

God's Plan for Women Is to...

God Teaches Women to Walk in His Word by...

God Delights in Women Who Are...

God Walks with Women...

God Encourages Each Woman to...

God Teaches a Woman How to...

God Blesses Women When They...

God Comforts Women as They Learn to...

God Gives Freely to Women...

God Helps Women to Grow by...

God Rejoices with Women When They...

Dynamic Women of Faith

God's Plan
for Women
Is to . . .

Worship Him

Give unto the LORD, O you mighty ones,
Give unto the LORD glory and strength.
Give unto the LORD the glory due to
    His name;
Worship the LORD in the beauty of holiness.

Psalm 29:1–2

Oh come, let us worship and bow down;
Let us kneel before the LORD our Maker.
For He is our God,
And we are the people of His pasture,
And the sheep of His hand.
Today, if you will hear His voice.

Psalm 95:6–7

The hour is coming, and now is, when the true worshipers will worship the Father in spirit and truth; for the Father is seeking such to worship Him. God is Spirit, and those who worship Him must worship in spirit and truth.

John 4:23–24

Oh, worship the LORD in the beauty of
    holiness!
Tremble before Him, all the earth.

Psalm 96:9

Then you will call upon Me and go and pray to Me, and I will listen to you. And you will seek Me and find Me, when you search for Me with all your heart.

Jeremiah 29:12–13

Seek the LORD and His strength;
Seek His face evermore!
Remember His marvelous works which
    He has done,
His wonders, and the judgments of
    His mouth.

1 Chronicles 16:11–12

Blessed are those who keep His testimonies,
Who seek Him with the whole heart!
With my whole heart I have sought You;
Oh, let me not wander from Your
    commandments!

Psalm 119:2, 10

Thus I will bless You while I live;
I will lift up my hands in Your name.
My soul shall be satisfied as with marrow
    and fatness,
And my mouth shall praise You with
    joyful lips.

Psalm 63:4–5

Obey Him

But be doers of the word, and not hearers only, deceiving yourselves.

James 1:22

If you love Me, keep My commandments.

John 14:15

Peter and the other apostles answered and said: "We ought to obey God rather than men."

Acts 5:29

Whoever comes to Me, and hears My sayings and does them, I will show you whom he is like: He is like a man building a house, who dug deep and laid the foundation on the rock. And when the flood arose, the stream beat vehemently against that house, and could not shake it, for it was founded on the rock. But he who heard and did nothing is like a man who built a house on the earth without a foundation, against which the stream beat vehemently; and immediately it fell. And the ruin of that house was great.

Luke 6:47–49

He who is faithful in what is least is faithful also in much; and he who is unjust in what is least is unjust also in much.

Luke 16:10

We have had human fathers who corrected us, and we paid them respect. Shall we not much more readily be in subjection to the Father of spirits and live? For they indeed for a few days chastened us as seemed best to them, but He for our profit, that we may be partakers of His holiness.

Hebrews 12:9–10

The world is passing away, and the lust of it; but he who does the will of God abides forever.

1 John 2:17

Now the just shall live by faith;
But if anyone draws back,
My soul has no pleasure in him.

Hebrews 10:38

Come to Him in Prayer

Let us therefore come boldly to the throne of grace, that we may obtain mercy and find grace to help in time of need.

Hebrews 4:16

Evening and morning and at noon
I will pray, and cry aloud,
And He shall hear my voice.

Psalm 55:17

Give ear, O LORD, to my prayer;
And attend to the voice of my supplications.
In the day of my trouble I will call upon You,
For You will answer me.

Psalm 86:6–7

For the eyes of the LORD are on the
    righteous,
And His ears are open to their prayers;
But the face of the LORD is against those
    who do evil.

1 Peter 3:12

Then He spoke a parable to them, that men always ought to pray and not lose heart.

Luke 18:1

When you pray, you shall not be like the hypocrites. For they love to pray standing in the synagogues and on the corners of the streets, that they may be seen by men. Assuredly, I say to you, they have their reward. But you, when you pray, go into your room, and when you have shut your door, pray to your Father who is in the secret place; and your Father who sees in secret will reward you openly.

Matthew 6:5–6

You will make your prayer to Him,
He will hear you,
And you will pay your vows.
You will also declare a thing,
And it will be established for you;
So light will shine on your ways.

Job 22:27–28

Let him ask in faith, with no doubting, for he who doubts is like a wave of the sea driven and tossed by the wind.

James 1:6

Listen to the Holy Spirit

For what man knows the things of a man except the spirit of the man which is in him? Even so no one knows the things of God except the Spirit of God. Now we have received, not the spirit of the world, but the Spirit who is from God, that we might know the things that have been freely given to us by God.

These things we also speak, not in words which man's wisdom teaches but which the Holy Spirit teaches, comparing spiritual things with spiritual.

1 Corinthians 2:11–13

For the Holy Spirit will teach you in that very hour what you ought to say.

Luke 12:12

Speaking the truth in love, may grow up in all things into Him who is the head—Christ—from whom the whole body, joined and knit together by what every joint supplies, according to the effective working by which every part does its share, causes growth of the body for the edifying of itself in love.

Do not grieve the Holy Spirit of God, by whom you were sealed for the day of redemption.

Ephesians 4:15–16, 30

You, beloved, building yourselves up on your most holy faith, praying in the Holy Spirit, keep yourselves in the love of God, looking for the mercy of our Lord Jesus Christ unto eternal life.

Jude 20–21

Nevertheless I tell you the truth. It is to your advantage that I go away; for if I do not go away, the Helper will not come to you; but if I depart, I will send Him to you. And when He has come, He will convict the world of sin, and of righteousness, and of judgment: of sin, because they do not believe in Me; of righteousness, because I go to My Father and you see Me no more; of judgment, because the ruler of this world is judged.

I still have many things to say to you, but you cannot bear them now.

John 16:7–12

Knowing this first, that no prophecy of Scripture is of any private interpretation, for prophecy never came by the will of man, but holy men of God spoke as they were moved by the Holy Spirit.

2 Peter 1:20–21

If the Spirit of Him who raised Jesus from the dead dwells in you, He who raised Christ from the dead will also give life to your mortal bodies through His Spirit who dwells in you.

The Spirit Himself bears witness with our spirit that we are children of God, and if children, then heirs—heirs of God and joint heirs with Christ, if indeed we suffer with Him, that we may also be glorified together.

For I consider that the sufferings of this present time are not worthy to be compared with the glory which shall be revealed in us.

Likewise the Spirit also helps in our weaknesses. For we do not know what we should pray for as we ought, but the Spirit Himself makes intercession for us with groanings which cannot be uttered. Now He who searches the hearts knows what the mind of the Spirit is, because He makes intercession for the saints according to the will of God.

Romans 8:11, 16–18, 26–27

But the Helper, the Holy Spirit, whom the Father will send in My name, He will teach you all things, and bring to your remembrance all things that I said to you.

John 14:26

Being assembled together with them, He commanded them not to depart from Jerusalem, but to wait for the Promise of the Father, "which," He said, "you have heard from Me; for John truly baptized with water, but you shall be baptized with the Holy Spirit not many days from now."

And He said to them, "It is not for you to know times or seasons which the Father has put in His own authority. But you shall receive power when the Holy Spirit has come upon you; and you shall be witnesses to Me in Jerusalem, and in all Judea and Samaria, and to the end of the earth."

Acts 1:4–5, 7–8

Not that we are sufficient of ourselves to think of anything as being from ourselves, but our sufficiency is from God, who also made us sufficient as ministers of the new covenant, not of the letter but of the Spirit; for the letter kills, but the Spirit gives life.

Now the Lord is the Spirit; and where the Spirit of the Lord is, there is liberty. But we all, with unveiled face, beholding as in a mirror the glory of the Lord, are being transformed into the same image from glory to glory, just as by the Spirit of the Lord.

2 Corinthians 3:5–6, 17–18

*God Teaches Women
to Walk
in His Word by . . .*

Praising His Might ✿

Praise the LORD!
Sing to the LORD a new song,
And His praise in the assembly of saints.

Psalm 149:1

Praise the LORD!
Oh, give thanks to the LORD, for He is good!
For His mercy endures forever.
Who can utter the mighty acts of the LORD?
Who can declare all His praise?

Psalm 106:1–2

Praise the LORD!
Praise, O servants of the LORD,
Praise the name of the LORD!
Blessed be the name of the LORD
From this time forth and forevermore!
From the rising of the sun to its going down
The LORD's name is to be praised.

Psalm 113:1–3

I will praise the name of God with a song,
And will magnify Him with thanksgiving.

Psalm 69:30

My heart is steadfast, O God, my heart
    is steadfast;
I will sing and give praise.
Awake, my glory!
Awake, lute and harp!
I will awaken the dawn.
I will praise You, O Lord, among the peoples;
I will sing to You among the nations.

Psalm 57:7–9

Praise the LORD!
Praise the LORD, O my soul!
While I live I will praise the LORD;
I will sing praises to my God while I have
    my being.

Psalm 146:1–2

Great is the LORD, and greatly to be praised
In the city of our God,
In His holy mountain.

Psalm 48:1

Every good gift and every perfect gift is from
above, and comes down from the Father of lights.

James 1:17

Because Your lovingkindness is better
    than life,
My lips shall praise You.
Thus I will bless You while I live;
I will lift up my hands in Your name.
My soul shall be satisfied as with marrow
    and fatness,
And my mouth shall praise You with
    joyful lips.

Psalm 63:3–5

Trusting His Power

It shall come to pass
That before they call, I will answer;
And while they are still speaking, I will hear.
Isaiah 65:24

You will keep him in perfect peace,
Whose mind is stayed on You,
Because he trusts in You.
Trust in the LORD forever,
For in YAH, the LORD, is everlasting strength.
Isaiah 26:3–4

Behold, God is my salvation,
I will trust and not be afraid;
For YAH, the LORD, is my strength and song;
He also has become my salvation.
Isaiah 12:2

The LORD is on my side;
I will not fear.
What can man do to me?
It is better to trust in the LORD
Than to put confidence in man.
Psalm 118:6, 8

In You, O LORD, I put my trust;
Let me never be put to shame.
For You are my hope, O Lord GOD;
You are my trust from my youth.
Let my mouth be filled with Your praise
And with Your glory all the day.
Psalm 71:1, 5, 8

Yes, we had the sentence of death in ourselves, that we should not trust in ourselves but in
God who raises the dead, who delivered us from so
great a death, and does deliver us; in whom we
trust that He will still deliver us.
2 Corinthians 1:9–10

He will not be afraid of evil tidings;
His heart is steadfast, trusting in the LORD.
His heart is established;
He will not be afraid,
Until he sees his desire upon his enemies.
Psalm 112:7–8

The salvation of the righteous is from
the LORD;
He is their strength in the time of trouble.
And the LORD shall help them and
deliver them;
He shall deliver them from the wicked,
And save them,
Because they trust in Him.
Psalm 37:39–40

Focusing on His Love

For thus says the Lord GOD, the Holy
    One of Israel:
"In returning and rest you shall be saved;
In quietness and confidence shall be
    your strength."

Isaiah 30:15

His work is honorable and glorious,
And His righteousness endures forever.
He has made His wonderful works to
    be remembered;
The LORD is gracious and full of
    compassion.

Psalm 111:3–4

We are always confident, knowing that while
we are at home in the body we are absent from the
Lord. For we walk by faith, not by sight.

2 Corinthians 5:6–7

Fear not, for I am with you;
Be not dismayed, for I am your God.
I will strengthen you,
Yes, I will help you,
I will uphold you with My righteous
    right hand.

Isaiah 41:10

God is our refuge and strength,
A very present help in trouble.
Therefore we will not fear,
Even though the earth be removed,
And though the mountains be carried
     into the midst of the sea;
Though its waters roar and be troubled,
Though the mountains shake with
     its swelling.

Psalm 46:1–3

Hungry and thirsty,
Their soul fainted in them.
Then they cried out to the LORD in
     their trouble,
And He delivered them out of their
     distresses.
And He led them forth by the right way,
That they might go to a city for a
     dwelling place.

Psalm 107:5–7

God has not given us a spirit of fear, but of
power and of love and of a sound mind.

Who has saved us and called us with a holy
calling, not according to our works, but according
to His own purpose and grace which was given to
us in Christ Jesus before time began.

2 Timothy 1:7, 9

Come to Me, all you who labor and are heavy laden, and I will give you rest. Take My yoke upon you and learn from Me, for I am gentle and lowly in heart, and you will find rest for your souls. For My yoke is easy and My burden is light.

Matthew 11:28–30

For He Himself has said, "I will never leave you nor forsake you."

Hebrews 13:5

I am the God of your father Abraham; do not fear, for I am with you.

Genesis 26:24

Praying for His Will 🌼

Evening and morning and at noon
I will pray, and cry aloud,
And He shall hear my voice.

Psalm 55:17

Now when Daniel knew that the writing was signed, he went home. And in his upper room, with his windows open toward Jerusalem, he knelt down on his knees three times that day, and prayed and gave thanks before his God, as was his custom since early days.

Daniel 6:10

Seven times a day I praise You,
Because of Your righteous judgments.

Psalm 119:164

I will meditate on Your precepts,
And contemplate Your ways.
I will delight myself in Your statutes;
I will not forget Your word.

Psalm 119:15–16

Your word is a lamp to my feet
And a light to my path.

Psalm 119:105

So then faith comes by hearing, and hearing by the word of God.

Romans 10:17

These are the ones sown on good ground, those who hear the word, accept it, and bear fruit: some thirtyfold, some sixty, and some a hundred.

Mark 4:20

The LORD is far from the wicked,
But He hears the prayer of the righteous.

Proverbs 15:29

Pray without ceasing.

1 Thessalonians 5:17

Following His Light

> For the commandment is a lamp,
> And the law a light;
> Reproofs of instruction are the way of life.
>
> *Proverbs 6:23*

> Be diligent to present yourself approved to God, a worker who does not need to be ashamed, rightly dividing the word of truth.
>
> *2 Timothy 2:15*

> Your word I have hidden in my heart,
> That I might not sin against You.
> Blessed are You, O LORD!
> Teach me Your statutes!
>
> *Psalm 119:11–12*

> For in Him we live and move and have our being, as also some of your own poets have said, "For we are also His offspring."
>
> *Acts 17:28*

> Whoever transgresses and does not abide in the doctrine of Christ does not have God. He who abides in the doctrine of Christ has both the Father and the Son.
>
> *2 John 1:9*

Draw near to God and He will draw near to you. Cleanse your hands, you sinners; and purify your hearts, you double-minded.

James 4:8

Jesus said to him, "If you can believe, all things are possible to him who believes."

Mark 9:23

Those who are Christ's have crucified the flesh with its passions and desires. If we live in the Spirit, let us also walk in the Spirit.

Galatians 5:24–25

Rejoicing Day and Night

How sweet are Your words to my taste,
Sweeter than honey to my mouth!

Psalm 119:103

The law of the LORD is perfect,
 converting the soul;
The testimony of the LORD is sure,
 making wise the simple;
The statutes of the LORD are right,
 rejoicing the heart;
The commandment of the LORD is pure,
 enlightening the eyes;
More to be desired are they than gold,
Yea, than much fine gold;
Sweeter also than honey and the honeycomb.

Psalm 19:7–8, 10

This Book of the Law shall not depart from your mouth, but you shall meditate in it day and night, that you may observe to do according to all that is written in it. For then you will make your way prosperous, and then you will have good success.

Joshua 1:8

I will meditate on Your precepts,
And contemplate Your ways.
I will delight myself in Your statutes;
I will not forget Your word.

Psalm 119:15–16

You put off, concerning your former conduct, the old man which grows corrupt according to the deceitful lusts, and be renewed in the spirit of your mind, and that you put on the new man which was created according to God, in true righteousness and holiness.

Ephesians 4:22–24

We do not lose heart. Even though our outward man is perishing, yet the inward man is being renewed day by day.

2 Corinthians 4:16

The LORD will command His lovingkindness
    in the daytime,
And in the night His song shall be
    with me—
A prayer to the God of my life.

Psalm 42:8

God Delights in
Women Who Are . . .

Seeking Him 🌸

When my father and my mother forsake me,
Then the LORD will take care of me.

Psalm 27:10

O God, You are my God;
Early will I seek You;
My soul thirsts for You;
My flesh longs for You
In a dry and thirsty land
Where there is no water.

Psalm 63:1

Seek the LORD and His strength;
Seek His face evermore!
Remember His marvelous works which
　　He has done,
His wonders, and the judgments of
　　His mouth.

1 Chronicles 16:11–12

If you confess with your mouth the Lord
Jesus and believe in your heart that God has raised
Him from the dead, you will be saved.

Romans 10:9

I love those who love me,
And those who seek me diligently will
    find me.

Proverbs 8:17

Till I come, give attention to reading, to
exhortation, to doctrine.

1 Timothy 4:13

There is a way that seems right to a man,
But its end is the way of death.

Proverbs 14:12

I sought the LORD, and He heard me,
And delivered me from all my fears.

Psalm 34:4

Always pursue what is good both for yourselves and for all.

1 Thessalonians 5:15

Confident of Him

> I will not leave you orphans; I will come to you.
>
> *John 14:18*

> I thank my God upon every remembrance of you.
>
> *Philippians 1:3*

> In You, O LORD, I put my trust;
> Let me never be put to shame.
> Deliver me in Your righteousness, and
> cause me to escape;
> Incline Your ear to me, and save me.
> For You are my hope, O Lord GOD;
> You are my trust from my youth.
>
> *Psalm 71:1– 2, 5*

> It is better to trust in the LORD
> Than to put confidence in man.
>
> *Psalm 118:8*

> The LORD shall preserve you from all evil;
> He shall preserve your soul.
> The LORD shall preserve your going out
> and your coming in
> From this time forth, and even forevermore.
>
> *Psalm 121:7–8*

Therefore submit to God. Resist the devil and he will flee from you.

James 4:7

Grace and peace be multiplied to you in the knowledge of God and of Jesus our Lord, as His divine power has given to us all things that pertain to life and godliness, through the knowledge of Him who called us by glory and virtue, by which have been given to us exceedingly great and precious promises, that through these you may be partakers of the divine nature, having escaped the corruption that is in the world through lust.

2 Peter 1:2–4

Who is he who overcomes the world, but he who believes that Jesus is the Son of God?

1 John 5:5

With men this is impossible, but with God all things are possible.

Matthew 19:26

Forgiven by Him 🌼

Now to Him who is able to keep you
    from stumbling,
And to present you faultless
Before the presence of His glory with
    exceeding joy,
To God our Savior,
Who alone is wise,
Be glory and majesty,
Dominion and power,
Both now and forever.

Jude 24–25

There is therefore now no condemnation to
those who are in Christ Jesus, who do not walk
according to the flesh, but according to the Spirit.
For the law of the Spirit of life in Christ Jesus has
made me free from the law of sin and death.

Romans 8:1–2

If we confess our sins, He is faithful and just
to forgive us our sins and to cleanse us from all
unrighteousness.

1 John 1:9

You have forgiven the iniquity of
    Your people;
You have covered all their sin.

Psalm 85:2

The Lord is faithful, who will establish you and guard you from the evil one.

2 Thessalonians 3:3

Now whom you forgive anything, I also forgive. For if indeed I have forgiven anything, I have forgiven that one for your sakes in the presence of Christ, lest Satan should take advantage of us; for we are not ignorant of his devices.

2 Corinthians 2:10–11

To him who overcomes I will grant to sit with Me on My throne, as I also overcame and sat down with My Father on His throne.

Revelation 3:21

The Lord will deliver me from every evil work and preserve me for His heavenly kingdom. To Him be glory forever and ever. Amen!

2 Timothy 4:18

Growing in Him

> I will instruct you and teach you in the
>   way you should go;
> I will guide you with My eye.
>
> *Psalm 32:8*

> This Book of the Law shall not depart from
> your mouth, but you shall meditate in it day and
> night, that you may observe to do according to all
> that is written in it. For then you will make your way
> prosperous, and then you will have good success.
>
> *Joshua 1:8*

> That we should no longer be children, tossed
> to and fro and carried about with every wind of
> doctrine, by the trickery of men, in the cunning
> craftiness of deceitful plotting, but, speaking the
> truth in love, may grow up in all things into Him
> who is the head—Christ.
>
> *Ephesians 4:14–15*

> Be doers of the word, and not hearers only,
> deceiving yourselves.
>
> *James 1:22*

> I am the vine, you are the branches. He who
> abides in Me, and I in him, bears much fruit; for
> without Me you can do nothing.
>
> *John 15:5*

O God, You are my God;
Early will I seek You;
My soul thirsts for You;
My flesh longs for You
In a dry and thirsty land
Where there is no water.
So I have looked for You in the sanctuary,
To see Your power and Your glory.
My soul shall be satisfied as with marrow
and fatness,
And my mouth shall praise You with
joyful lips.
When I remember You on my bed,
I meditate on You in the night watches.
Because You have been my help,
Therefore in the shadow of Your wings I
will rejoice.

Psalm 63:1–2, 5–7

You did not choose Me, but I chose you and appointed you that you should go and bear fruit, and that your fruit should remain, that whatever you ask the Father in My name He may give you.

John 15:16

For in Him we live and move and have our being, as also some of your own poets have said, "For we are also His offspring."

Acts 17:28

Serving Him 🌸

If it seems evil to you to serve the LORD, choose for yourselves this day whom you will serve, whether the gods which your fathers served that were on the other side of the River, or the gods of the Amorites, in whose land you dwell. But as for me and my house, we will serve the LORD.

Joshua 24:15

If anyone serves Me, let him follow Me; and where I am, there My servant will be also. If anyone serves Me, him My Father will honor.

John 12:26

Then Jesus said to him, "Away with you, Satan! For it is written, 'You shall worship the LORD your God, and Him only you shall serve.'"

Matthew 4:10

So the people asked him, saying, "What shall we do then?"

He answered and said to them, "He who has two tunics, let him give to him who has none; and he who has food, let him do likewise."

Luke 3:10–11

By this all will know that you are My disciples, if you have love for one another.

John 13:35

Command those who are rich in this present age not to be haughty, nor to trust in uncertain riches but in the living God, who gives us richly all things to enjoy. Let them do good, that they be rich in good works, ready to give, willing to share, storing up for themselves a good foundation for the time to come, that they may lay hold on eternal life.

1 Timothy 6:17–19

Let each one examine his own work, and then he will have rejoicing in himself alone, and not in another. For each one shall bear his own load.

Let him who is taught the word share in all good things with him who teaches.

Let us not grow weary while doing good, for in due season we shall reap if we do not lose heart.

Galatians 6:4–6, 9

The people said to Joshua, "The LORD our God we will serve, and His voice we will obey!"

Joshua 24:24

Showing Him to Others 🌿

Now by this we know that we know Him, if we keep His commandments.

Whoever keeps His word, truly the love of God is perfected in him. By this we know that we are in Him.

1 John 2:3, 5

Having been justified by faith, we have peace with God through our Lord Jesus Christ, through whom also we have access by faith into this grace in which we stand, and rejoice in hope of the glory of God. And not only that, but we also glory in tribulations, knowing that tribulation produces perseverance; and perseverance, character; and character, hope.

Romans 5:1–4

Finally, my brethren, be strong in the Lord and in the power of His might. Put on the whole armor of God, that you may be able to stand against the wiles of the devil.

Ephesians 6:10–11

That which we have seen and heard we declare to you, that you also may have fellowship with us; and truly our fellowship is with the Father and with His Son Jesus Christ.

1 John 1:3

Someone will say, "You have faith, and I have works." Show me your faith without your works, and I will show you my faith by my works.

Do you see that faith was working together with his works, and by works faith was made perfect?

James 2:18, 22

"Woe to the rebellious children," says the
   LORD,
"Who take counsel, but not of Me,
   And who devise plans, but not of My Spirit,
   That they may add sin to sin.

Isaiah 30:1

My beloved brethren, let every man be swift to hear, slow to speak, slow to wrath; for the wrath of man does not produce the righteousness of God.

Therefore lay aside all filthiness and overflow of wickedness, and receive with meekness the implanted word, which is able to save your souls.

Pure and undefiled religion before God and the Father is this: to visit orphans and widows in their trouble, and to keep oneself unspotted from the world.

James 1:19–21, 27

Now these are the ones sown among thorns; they are the ones who hear the word, and the cares of this world, the deceitfulness of riches, and the desires for other things entering in choke the word, and it becomes unfruitful. But these are the ones sown on good ground, those who hear the word, accept it, and bear fruit: some thirtyfold, some sixty, and some a hundred.

Mark 4:18–20

Though now you do not see Him, yet believing, you rejoice with joy inexpressible and full of glory.

1 Peter 1:18

We speak, not as pleasing men, but who tests our hearts.

1 Thessalonians 2:4

God Walks with
Women . . .

Through Heartache

> He heals the brokenhearted
> And binds up their wounds.
>
> *Psalm 147:3*

> A man's heart plans his way,
> But the LORD directs his steps.
> The lot is cast into the lap,
> But its every decision is from the LORD.
>
> *Proverbs 16:9, 33*

> The LORD is near to those who have a
>   broken heart,
> And saves such as have a contrite spirit.
> Many are the afflictions of the righteous,
> But the LORD delivers him out of them all.
>
> *Psalm 34:18–19*

Come to Me, all you who labor and are heavy laden, and I will give you rest. Take My yoke upon you and learn from Me, for I am gentle and lowly in heart, and you will find rest for your souls.

> *Matthew 11:28–29*

"Now I will rise," says the LORD;
"Now I will be exalted,
  Now I will lift Myself up."

Isaiah 33:10

The LORD also will be a refuge for
    the oppressed,
A refuge in times of trouble.
And those who know Your name will
    put their trust in You;
For You, LORD, have not forsaken those
    who seek You.

Psalm 9:9–10

In the day when I cried out, You
    answered me,
And made me bold with strength in my soul.

Psalm 138:3

The LORD will guide you continually,
And satisfy your soul in drought,
And strengthen your bones;
You shall be like a watered garden,
And like a spring of water, whose waters
    do not fail.

Isaiah 58:11

Through Adversity

The fear of man brings a snare,
But whoever trusts in the LORD shall be safe.

Proverbs 29:25

Through God we will do valiantly,
For it is He who shall tread down our enemies.

Psalm 60:12

Beloved, do not think it strange concerning the fiery trial which is to try you, as though some strange thing happened to you; but rejoice to the extent that you partake of Christ's sufferings, that when His glory is revealed, you may also be glad with exceeding joy.

1 Peter 4:12–13

Yes, may you see your children's children.
Peace be upon Israel!

Psalm 128:6

Now thanks be to God who always leads us in triumph in Christ, and through us diffuses the fragrance of His knowledge in every place.

2 Corinthians 2:14

My heart is steadfast, O God, my heart
    is steadfast;
I will sing and give praise.

Psalm 57:7

He said to me, "My grace is sufficient for you, for My strength is made perfect in weakness." Therefore most gladly I will rather boast in my infirmities, that the power of Christ may rest upon me.

2 Corinthians 12:9

The LORD will perfect that which
    concerns me;
Your mercy, O LORD, endures forever;
Do not forsake the works of Your hands.

Psalm 138:8

Through Danger

My soul, wait silently for God alone,
For my expectation is from Him.
He only is my rock and my salvation;
He is my defense;
I shall not be moved.
In God is my salvation and my glory;
The rock of my strength,
And my refuge, is in God.

Psalm 62:5–7

Do not be a terror to me;
You are my hope in the day of doom.

Jeremiah 17:17

When you pass through the waters, I will
    be with you;
And through the rivers, they shall not
    overflow you.
When you walk through the fire, you
    shall not be burned,
Nor shall the flame scorch you.

Isaiah 43:2

Keep me as the apple of Your eye;
Hide me under the shadow of Your wings.

Psalm 17:8

Yea, though I walk through the valley of
     the shadow of death,
I will fear no evil;
For You are with me;
Your rod and Your staff, they comfort me.

Psalm 23:4

You number my wanderings;
Put my tears into Your bottle;
Are they not in Your book?
In God I have put my trust;
I will not be afraid.
What can man do to me?

Psalm 56:8, 11

He raises the poor out of the dust,
And lifts the needy out of the ash heap,
He grants the barren woman a home,
Like a joyful mother of children.
Praise the LORD!

Psalm 113:7, 9

For in the time of trouble
He shall hide me in His pavilion;
In the secret place of His tabernacle
He shall hide me;
He shall set me high upon a rock.

Psalm 27:5

Through Impatience

> My soul waits for the Lord
> More than those who watch for the
>   morning—
> Yes, more than those who watch for
>   the morning.

Psalm 130:6

My brethren, count it all joy when you fall into various trials, knowing that the testing of your faith produces patience. But let patience have its perfect work, that you may be perfect and complete, lacking nothing.

James 1:2–4

Be patient, brethren, until the coming of the Lord. See how the farmer waits for the precious fruit of the earth, waiting patiently for it until it receives the early and latter rain. You also be patient. Establish your hearts, for the coming of the Lord is at hand.

James 5:7–8

He said, "My Presence will go with you, and I will give you rest."

Exodus 33:14

Wait on the LORD;
Be of good courage,
And He shall strengthen your heart;
Wait, I say, on the LORD!

Psalm 27:14

Those who wait on the LORD
Shall renew their strength;
They shall mount up with wings like eagles,
They shall run and not be weary,
They shall walk and not faint.

Isaiah 40:31

I cried to the LORD with my voice,
And He heard me from His holy hill.
I lay down and slept;
I awoke, for the LORD sustained me.

Psalm 3:4–5

So, after he had patiently endured, he obtained the promise.

Hebrews 6:15

Through Disappointment 🌸

> LORD, I cry out to You;
> Make haste to me!
> Give ear to my voice when I cry out to You.
> Let my prayer be set before You as incense,
> The lifting up of my hands as the evening
>   sacrifice.
>
> *Psalm 141:1–2*

> Many people shall come and say,
> "Come, and let us go up to the mountain
>   of the LORD,
> To the house of the God of Jacob;
> He will teach us His ways,
> And we shall walk in His paths."
> For out of Zion shall go forth the law,
> And the word of the LORD from Jerusalem.
>
> *Isaiah 2:3*

> Fight the good fight of faith, lay hold on eternal life, to which you were also called and have confessed the good confession in the presence of many witnesses.
>
> *1 Timothy 6:12*

> Though He was a Son, yet He learned obedience by the things which He suffered.
>
> *Hebrews 5:8*

I have fought the good fight, I have finished the race, I have kept the faith. Finally, there is laid up for me the crown of righteousness, which the Lord, the righteous Judge, will give to me on that Day, and not to me only but also to all who have loved His appearing.

2 Timothy 4:7–8

Now godliness with contentment is great gain. For we brought nothing into this world, and it is certain we can carry nothing out. And having food and clothing, with these we shall be content.

1 Timothy 6:6–8

I know that whatever God does,
It shall be forever.
Nothing can be added to it,
And nothing taken from it.
God does it, that men should fear before
　　Him.

Ecclesiastes 3:14

The wisdom that is from above is first pure, then peaceable, gentle, willing to yield, full of mercy and good fruits, without partiality and without hypocrisy.

James 3:17

For this is commendable, if because of conscience toward God one endures grief, suffering wrongfully. For what credit is it if, when you are beaten for your faults, you take it patiently? But when you do good and suffer, if you take it patiently, this is commendable before God.

1 Peter 2:19–20

May our Lord Jesus Christ . . . comfort your hearts and establish you in every good word and work.

2 Thessalonians 2:16

Love bears all things, believes all things, hopes all things, endures all things.

1 Corinthians 13:7

Through Failure

He who loves his life will lose it, and he who hates his life in this world will keep it for eternal life.

John 12:25

Set your mind on things above, not on things on the earth.

Colossians 3:2

Command those who are rich in this present age not to be haughty, nor to trust in uncertain riches but in the living God, who gives us richly all things to enjoy. Let them do good, that they be rich in good works, ready to give, willing to share, storing up for themselves a good foundation for the time to come, that they may lay hold on eternal life.

1 Timothy 6:17–19

Listen to counsel and receive instruction, That you may be wise in your latter days.

Proverbs 19:20

For I considered all this in my heart, so that I could declare it all: that the righteous and the wise and their works are in the hand of God. People know neither love nor hatred by anything they see before them.

Ecclesiastes 9:1

You are a chosen generation, a royal priest-hood, a holy nation, His own special people, that you may proclaim the praises of Him who called you out of darkness into His marvelous light.

1 Peter 2:9

He has not dealt with us according to
     our sins,
Nor punished us according to our iniquities.
For as the heavens are high above the earth,
So great is His mercy toward those who
     fear Him;
As far as the east is from the west,
So far has He removed our transgressions
     from us.

Psalm 103:10–12

Cast your burden on the LORD,
And He shall sustain you;
He shall never permit the righteous to
     be moved.

Psalm 55:22

God Encourages Each Woman to . . .

Cherish Being a Friend 🌸

Let brotherly love continue. Do not forget to entertain strangers, for by so doing some have unwittingly entertained angels.

Hebrews 13:1–2

A friend loves at all times,
And a brother is born for adversity.

Proverbs 17:17

This is My commandment, that you love one another as I have loved you. Greater love has no one than this, than to lay down one's life for his friends.

John 15:12–13

If one member suffers, all the members suffer with it; or if one member is honored, all the members rejoice with it.

1 Corinthians 12:26

Two are better than one,
Because they have a good reward for
their labor.

Ecclesiastes 4:9

Everyone helped his neighbor,
And said to his brother,
"Be of good courage!"

Isaiah 41:6

For whoever does the will of My Father in heaven is My brother and sister and mother.

Matthew 12:50

For as the body is one and has many members, but all the members of that one body, being many, are one body, so also is Christ.

1 Corinthians 12:12

Through love, serve one another.

Galatians 5:13

Let all that you do be done with love.

1 Corinthians 16:14

Give to Others with Grace

Let us not grow weary while doing good, for in due season we shall reap if we do not lose heart.
Galatians 6:9

Give, and it will be given to you: good measure, pressed down, shaken together, and running over will be put into your bosom. For with the same measure that you use, it will be measured back to you.
Luke 6:38

She extends her hand to the poor,
Yes, she reaches out her hands to the needy.
Proverbs 31:20

He who gives to the poor will not lack,
But he who hides his eyes will have
many curses.
Proverbs 28:27

Defend the poor and fatherless;
Do justice to the afflicted and needy.
Deliver the poor and needy;
Free them from the hand of the wicked.
Psalm 82:3–4

By this we know love, because He laid down His life for us. And we also ought to lay down our lives for the brethren. But whoever has this world's goods, and sees his brother in need, and shuts up his heart from him, how does the love of God abide in him?

1 John 3:16–17

Whoever gives one of these little ones only a cup of cold water in the name of a disciple, assuredly, I say to you, he shall by no means lose his reward.

Matthew 10:42

What does the LORD require of you but to do justly, to love mercy, and to walk humbly with your God?

Micah 6:8

Be tenderhearted, be courteous . . . that you may inherit a blessing.

1 Peter 3:9

Live a Life of Service ✿

He who does not love does not know God, for God is love.

1 John 4:8

Now, little children, abide in Him, that when He appears, we may have confidence and not be ashamed before Him at His coming.

1 John 2:28

A new commandment I give to you, that you love one another; as I have loved you, that you also love one another. By this all will know that you are My disciples, if you have love for one another.

John 13:34–35

Whoever desires to be first among you, let him be your slave—just as the Son of Man did not come to be served, but to serve, and to give His life a ransom for many.

Matthew 20:27–28

For you, brethren, have been called to liberty; only do not use liberty as an opportunity for the flesh, but through love serve one another.

Galatians 5:13

As each one has received a gift, minister it to one another, as good stewards of the manifold grace of God. If anyone speaks, let him speak as the oracles of God. If anyone ministers, let him do it as with the ability which God supplies, that in all things God may be glorified through Jesus Christ, to whom belong the glory and the dominion forever and ever.

1 Peter 4:10–11

Whatever you do, do it heartily, as to the Lord and not to men, knowing that from the Lord you will receive the reward of the inheritance; for you serve the Lord Christ. But he who does wrong will be repaid for what he has done, and there is no partiality.

Colossians 3:23–25

He who is faithful in what is least is faithful also in much; and he who is unjust in what is least is unjust also in much. Therefore if you have not been faithful in the unrighteous mammon, who will commit to your trust the true riches? And if you have not been faithful in what is another man's, who will give you what is your own?

No servant can serve two masters; for either he will hate the one and love the other, or else he will be loyal to the one and despise the other. You cannot serve God and mammon.

Luke 16:10–13

Offer Encouragement

Rejoice with those who rejoice, and weep with those who weep. Be of the same mind toward one another. Do not set your mind on high things, but associate with the humble. Do not be wise in your own opinion.

Romans 12:15–16

Therefore comfort each other and edify one another, just as you also are doing.

1 Thessalonians 5:11

Therefore let us pursue the things which make for peace and the things by which one may edify another.

Romans 14:19

Let us consider one another in order to stir up love and good works, not forsaking the assembling of ourselves together, as is the manner of some, but exhorting one another, and so much the more as you see the Day approaching.

Hebrews 10:24–25

If we walk in the light as He is in the light, we have fellowship with one another, and the blood of Jesus Christ His Son cleanses us from all sin.

1 John 1:7

If then you were raised with Christ, seek those things which are above, where Christ is, sitting at the right hand of God. Set your mind on things above, not on things on the earth.

Colossians 3:1–2

You are my hiding place;
You shall preserve me from trouble;
You shall surround me with songs of
    deliverance.

Psalm 32:7

Do not fear, little flock, for it is your Father's good pleasure to give you the kingdom.

Luke 12:32

May the Lord of peace Himself give you peace always in every way.

2 Thessalonians 3:16

God has sent His only begotten Son into the world, that we might live through Him.

1 John 4:9

Pray for One Another

Behold, I am the LORD, the God of all flesh. Is there anything too hard for Me?

Jeremiah 32:27

Let this mind be in you which was also in Christ Jesus.

Philippians 2:5

For the eyes of the LORD are on the
        righteous,
And His ears are open to their prayers;
But the face of the LORD is against those
        who do evil.
And who is he who will harm you if you become followers of what is good?

1 Peter 3:12–13

Rejoice always, pray without ceasing, in everything give thanks; for this is the will of God in Christ Jesus for you.

1 Thessalonians 5:16–18

Take the helmet of salvation, and the sword of the Spirit, which is the word of God; praying always with all prayer and supplication in the Spirit, being watchful to this end with all perseverance and supplication for all the saints.

Ephesians 6:17–18

You are of God, little children, and have overcome them, because He who is in you is greater than he who is in the world.

1 John 4:4

Depart from me, all you workers of iniquity;
For the LORD has heard the voice of
    my weeping.
The LORD has heard my supplication;
The LORD will receive my prayer.

Psalm 6:8–9

Give ear, O LORD, to my prayer;
And attend to the voice of my supplications.
In the day of my trouble I will call upon You,
For You will answer me.

Psalm 86:6–7

Now this is the confidence that we have in Him, that if we ask anything according to His will, He hears us. And if we know that He hears us, whatever we ask, we know that we have the petitions that we have asked of Him.

1 John 5:14–15

Celebrate with Joy 🌸

I will praise You, O LORD, with my
    whole heart;
I will tell of all Your marvelous works.
I will be glad and rejoice in You;
I will sing praise to Your name,
    O Most High.

Psalm 9:1–2

It will be said in that day:
"Behold, this is our God;
We have waited for Him, and He will save us.
This is the LORD;
We have waited for Him;
We will be glad and rejoice in His salvation."

Isaiah 25:9

I will sing of the mercies of the LORD forever;
With my mouth will I make known
    Your faithfulness to all generations.

Psalm 89:1

I will delight myself in Your statutes;
I will not forget Your word.
Make me understand the way of Your precepts;
So shall I meditate on Your wonderful works.

Psalm 119:16, 27

A merry heart makes a cheerful countenance,
But by sorrow of the heart the spirit is broken.

Proverbs 15:13

Thus says the LORD: "Again there shall be heard in this place—of which you say, 'It is desolate, without man and without beast'—in the cities of Judah, in the streets of Jerusalem that are desolate, without man and without inhabitant and without beast, the voice of joy and the voice of gladness, the voice of the bridegroom and the voice of the bride, the voice of those who will say:
'Praise the Lord of hosts,
For the Lord is good,
For His mercy endures forever'—
and of those who will bring the sacrifice of praise into the house of the LORD. For I will cause the captives of the land to return as at the first," says the LORD.

Jeremiah 33:10–11

King Hezekiah and the leaders commanded the Levites to sing praise to the LORD with the words of David and of Asaph the seer. So they sang praises with gladness, and they bowed their heads and worshiped.

2 Chronicles 29:30

Blessed are the people who know the joyful sound!

Psalm 89:15

The LORD your God in your midst,
The Mighty One, will save;
He will rejoice over you with gladness,
He will quiet you with His love,
He will rejoice over you with singing.

Zephaniah 3:17

Let them shout for joy and be glad,
Who favor my righteous cause;
And let them say continually,
"Let the LORD be magnified,
Who has pleasure in the prosperity of
    His servant."
And my tongue shall speak of Your
    righteousness
And of Your praise all the day long.

Psalm 35:27–28

Bow down Your heavens, O LORD, and
    come down;
Touch the mountains, and they shall smoke.

Psalm 144:5

God Teaches a Woman How to . . .

Trust Him Completely

Beloved, do not believe every spirit, but test the spirits, whether they are of God; because many false prophets have gone out into the world.

1 John 4:1

The LORD is your keeper;
The LORD is your shade at your right hand.
The LORD shall preserve you from all evil;
He shall preserve your soul.
The LORD shall preserve your going out
    and your coming in
From this time forth, and even forevermore.

Psalm 121:5, 7–8

We have such trust through Christ toward God. Not that we are sufficient of ourselves to think of anything as being from ourselves, but our sufficiency is from God.

2 Corinthians 3:4–5

When I saw Him, I fell at His feet as dead. But He laid His right hand on me, saying to me, "Do not be afraid; I am the First and the Last. I am He who lives, and was dead, and behold, I am alive forevermore. Amen. And I have the keys of Hades and of Death."

Revelation 1:17–18

The LORD is my shepherd;
I shall not want.
He makes me to lie down in green pastures;
He leads me beside the still waters.
He restores my soul;
He leads me in the paths of righteousness
For His name's sake.
Yea, though I walk through the valley of
      the shadow of death,
I will fear no evil;
For You are with me;
Your rod and Your staff, they comfort me.

Psalm 23:1–4

My help comes from the LORD,
Who made heaven and earth.
He will not allow your foot to be moved;
He who keeps you will not slumber.

Psalm 121:2–3

I will say of the LORD, "He is my refuge
      and my fortress;
My God, in Him I will trust."
Surely He shall deliver you from the snare
      of the fowler
And from the perilous pestilence.
He shall cover you with His feathers,
And under His wings you shall take refuge;
His truth shall be your shield and buckler.

Psalm 91:2–4

Hold On to Faith

For there are three that bear witness in heaven: the Father, the Word, and the Holy Spirit; and these three are one.

1 John 5:7

Let us hold fast the confession of our hope without wavering, for He who promised is faithful.

Hebrews 10:23

Have I not commanded you? Be strong and of good courage; do not be afraid, nor be dismayed, for the LORD your God is with you wherever you go.

Joshua 1:9

For with God nothing will be impossible.

Luke 1:37

Beloved, while I was very diligent to write to you concerning our common salvation, I found it necessary to write to you exhorting you to contend earnestly for the faith which was once for all delivered to the saints.

Jude 3

For we walk by faith, not by sight.

2 Corinthians 5:7

Having shod your feet with the preparation of the gospel of peace; above all, taking the shield of faith with which you will be able to quench all the fiery darts of the wicked one.

Ephesians 6:15–16

You, beloved, building yourselves up on your most holy faith, praying in the Holy Spirit, keep yourselves in the love of God, looking for the mercy of our Lord Jesus Christ unto eternal life.

Jude 20–21

Be steadfast, immovable, always abounding in the work of the Lord.

1 Corinthians 15:58

To Him who is able to keep you from stumbling . . . be glory and majesty.

Jude 24–25

Have Joy in Him

> I say to you that likewise there will be more joy in heaven over one sinner who repents than over ninety-nine just persons who need no repentance.
>
> *Luke 15:7*

> This is the day the LORD has made;
> We will rejoice and be glad in it.
>
> *Psalm 118:24*

> These things I have spoken to you, that My joy may remain in you, and that your joy may be full. This is My commandment, that you love one another as I have loved you.
>
> *John 15:11–12*

> Create in me a clean heart, O God,
> And renew a steadfast spirit within me.
> Do not cast me away from Your presence,
> And do not take Your Holy Spirit from me.
> Restore to me the joy of Your salvation,
> And uphold me by Your generous Spirit.
>
> *Psalm 51:10–12*

> Let us come before His presence
>   with thanksgiving;
> Let us shout joyfully to Him with psalms.
>
> *Psalm 95:2*

Because Your lovingkindness is better
    than life,
My lips shall praise You.
Thus I will bless You while I live;
I will lift up my hands in Your name.
My soul shall be satisfied as with marrow
    and fatness,
And my mouth shall praise You with
    joyful lips.

Psalm 63:3–5

The kingdom of God is not eating and drinking, but righteousness and peace and joy in the Holy Spirit.

Romans 14:17

A merry heart makes a cheerful countenance,
But by sorrow of the heart the spirit is
    broken.

Proverbs 15:13

Oh, satisfy us early with Your mercy, that we may rejoice and be glad all our days!

Psalm 90:14

Center Her Life in Him

> Behold, all those who were incensed
> against you
> Shall be ashamed and disgraced;
> They shall be as nothing,
> And those who strive with you shall perish.
> You shall seek them and not find them—
> Those who contended with you.
> Those who war against you
> Shall be as nothing,
> As a nonexistent thing.
> For I, the LORD your God, will hold
> your right hand,
> Saying to you, "Fear not, I will help you."
> *Isaiah 41:11–13*

Let the word of Christ dwell in you richly in all wisdom, teaching and admonishing one another in psalms and hymns and spiritual songs, singing with grace in your hearts to the Lord.

Colossians 3:16

There is therefore now no condemnation to those who are in Christ Jesus, who do not walk according to the flesh, but according to the Spirit. For the law of the Spirit of life in Christ Jesus has made me free from the law of sin and death.

Romans 8:1–2

I sought the LORD, and He heard me,
And delivered me from all my fears.

Psalm 34:4

I will sing to the LORD as long as I live;
I will sing praise to my God while I have
    my being.
May my meditation be sweet to Him;
I will be glad in the LORD.

Psalm 104:33–34

Teaching us that, denying ungodliness and worldly lusts, we should live soberly, righteously, and godly in the present age, looking for the blessed hope and glorious appearing of our great God and Savior Jesus Christ.

Titus 2:12–13

I have been crucified with Christ; it is no longer I who live, but Christ lives in me; and the life which I now live in the flesh I live by faith in the Son of God, who loved me and gave Himself for me.

Galatians 2:20

My voice You shall hear in the morning,
    O LORD;
In the morning I will direct it to You,
And I will look up.

Psalm 5:3

Rest in His Protection

The LORD is my light and my salvation;
Whom shall I fear?
The LORD is the strength of my life;
Of whom shall I be afraid?
When the wicked came against me
To eat up my flesh,
My enemies and foes,
They stumbled and fell.
Though an army may encamp against me,
My heart shall not fear;
Though war may rise against me,
In this I will be confident.
One thing I have desired of the LORD,
That will I seek:
That I may dwell in the house of the LORD
All the days of my life,
To behold the beauty of the LORD,
And to inquire in His temple.
For in the time of trouble
He shall hide me in His pavilion;
In the secret place of His tabernacle
He shall hide me;
He shall set me high upon a rock.

Psalm 27:1–5

Whoever listens to me will dwell safely,
And will be secure, without fear of evil.

Proverbs 1:33

I cry out to the LORD with my voice;
With my voice to the LORD I make my
supplication.
I pour out my complaint before Him;
I declare before Him my trouble.

Psalm 142:1–2

The LORD is your keeper;
The LORD is your shade at your right hand.
The sun shall not strike you by day,
Nor the moon by night.
The LORD shall preserve you from all evil;
He shall preserve your soul.
The LORD shall preserve your going out
and your coming in
From this time forth, and even forevermore.

Psalm 121:5–8

"No weapon formed against you shall
prosper,
And every tongue which rises against you
in judgment
You shall condemn.
This is the heritage of the servants of
the LORD,
And their righteousness is from Me,"
Says the LORD.

Isaiah 54:17

I will both lie down in peace, and sleep;
For You alone, O LORD, make me dwell
    in safety.

Psalm 4:8

When you pass through the waters, I will
    be with you;
And through the rivers, they shall not
    overflow you.
When you walk through the fire, you
    shall not be burned,
Nor shall the flame scorch you.

Isaiah 43:2

May He send you help from the sanctuary,
And strengthen you out of Zion.

Psalm 20:2

You alone, O LORD, make me dwell in safety.

Psalm 4:8

The Lord is faithful, who will establish you
and guard you from the evil one.

2 Thessalonians 3:3

Obtain His Promises

Now this is the confidence that we have in Him, that if we ask anything according to His will, He hears us. And if we know that He hears us, whatever we ask, we know that we have the petitions that we have asked of Him.

1 John 5:14–15

If you diligently heed the voice of the LORD your God and do what is right in His sight, give ear to His commandments and keep all His statutes, I will put none of the diseases on you which I have brought on the Egyptians. For I am the LORD who heals you.

Exodus 15:26

Seek first the kingdom of God and His righteousness, and all these things shall be added to you.

Matthew 6:33

Do not become sluggish, but imitate those who through faith and patience inherit the promises.

Hebrews 6:12

Let us hold fast the confession of our hope without wavering, for He who promised is faithful.

Hebrews 10:23

By which have been given to us exceedingly great and precious promises, that through these you may be partakers of the divine nature, having escaped the corruption that is in the world through lust.

But also for this very reason, giving all diligence, add to your faith virtue, to virtue knowledge, to knowledge self-control, to self-control perseverance, to perseverance godliness, to godliness brotherly kindness, and to brotherly kindness love. For if these things are yours and abound, you will be neither barren nor unfruitful in the knowledge of our Lord Jesus Christ.

2 Peter 1:4–8

Now faith is the substance of things hoped for, the evidence of things not seen.

Without faith it is impossible to please Him, for he who comes to God must believe that He is, and that He is a rewarder of those who diligently seek Him.

By faith Sarah herself also received strength to conceive seed, and she bore a child when she was past the age, because she judged Him faithful who had promised.

Hebrews 11:1, 6, 11

For with God nothing will be impossible.
Luke 1:37

God Blesses Women
When They . . .

Trust in His Power

> In the LORD I put my trust;
> How can you say to my soul,
> "Flee as a bird to your mountain"?
> For look! The wicked bend their bow,
> They make ready their arrow on the string,
> That they may shoot secretly at the upright
>   in heart.
> If the foundations are destroyed,
> What can the righteous do?
> The LORD is in His holy temple,
> The LORD's throne is in heaven;
> His eyes behold,
> His eyelids test the sons of men.
> The LORD tests the righteous,
> But the wicked and the one who loves
>   violence His soul hates.
> Upon the wicked He will rain coals;
> Fire and brimstone and a burning wind
> Shall be the portion of their cup.
> For the LORD is righteous,
> He loves righteousness;
> His countenance beholds the upright.
>
> *Psalm 11:1–7*

> Trust in Him at all times, you people;
> Pour out your heart before Him;
> God is a refuge for us.
>
> *Psalm 62:8*

Those who trust in the LORD
Are like Mount Zion,
Which cannot be moved, but abides forever.
As the mountains surround Jerusalem,
So the LORD surrounds His people
From this time forth and forever.
For the scepter of wickedness shall not rest
On the land allotted to the righteous,
Lest the righteous reach out their hands
    to iniquity.
Do good, O LORD, to those who are good,
And to those who are upright in their hearts.
As for such as turn aside to their crooked
    ways,
The LORD shall lead them away
With the workers of iniquity.
Peace be upon Israel!

Psalm 125:1–5

For You will light my lamp;
The LORD my God will enlighten my
    darkness.
For by You I can run against a troop,
By my God I can leap over a wall.
As for God, His way is perfect;
The word of the LORD is proven;
He is a shield to all who trust in Him.

Psalm 18:28–30

Whenever I am afraid,
I will trust in You.
In God (I will praise His word),
In God I have put my trust;
I will not fear.
What can flesh do to me?

Psalm 56:3–4

LORD, how they have increased who
    trouble me!
Many are they who rise up against me.
Many are they who say of me,
"There is no help for him in God."
But You, O LORD, are a shield for me,
My glory and the One who lifts up my head.
I cried to the LORD with my voice,
And He heard me from His holy hill.
I lay down and slept;
I awoke, for the LORD sustained me.
I will not be afraid of ten thousands
    of people
Who have set themselves against me
    all around.
Arise, O LORD;
Save me, O my God!
For You have struck all my enemies on
    the cheekbone;
You have broken the teeth of the ungodly.
Salvation belongs to the LORD.
Your blessing is upon Your people.

Psalm 3:1–8

In God I have put my trust;
I will not be afraid.
What can man do to me?
Vows made to You are binding upon me,
    O God;
I will render praises to You.

Psalm 56:11–12

But You are holy,
Enthroned in the praises of Israel.
Our fathers trusted in You;
They trusted, and You delivered them.

Psalm 22:3–4

He shall cover you with His feathers, and
under His wings you shall take refuge.

Psalm 91:4

Praise His Goodness

Let the saints be joyful in glory;
Let them sing aloud on their beds.
Let the high praises of God be in
    their mouth,
And a two-edged sword in their hand.

Psalm 149:5–6

My heart is steadfast, O God, my heart
    is steadfast;
I will sing and give praise.
Awake, my glory!
Awake, lute and harp!
I will awaken the dawn.
I will praise You, O Lord, among the peoples;
I will sing to You among the nations.

Psalm 57:7–9

Praise Him with loud cymbals;
Praise Him with clashing cymbals!
Let everything that has breath praise
    the LORD.
Praise the LORD!

Psalm 150:5–6

Because Your lovingkindness is better
    than life,
My lips shall praise You.
Thus I will bless You while I live;
I will lift up my hands in Your name.

Psalm 63:3–4

Oh, give thanks to the LORD, for He is good!
For His mercy endures forever.
Oh, give thanks to the God of gods!
For His mercy endures forever.
Oh, give thanks to the Lord of lords!
For His mercy endures forever:
To Him who alone does great wonders,
For His mercy endures forever.

Psalm 136:1–4

In God (I will praise His word),
In the LORD (I will praise His word).

Psalm 56:10

I will bless the LORD at all times;
His praise shall continually be in my mouth.

Psalm 34:1

Whoever offers praise glorifies Me;
And to him who orders his conduct aright
I will show the salvation of God.

Psalm 50:23

Hope in His Faithfulness 🌼

We are hard pressed on every side, yet not crushed; we are perplexed, but not in despair; persecuted, but not forsaken; struck down, but not destroyed—always carrying about in the body the dying of the Lord Jesus, that the life of Jesus also may be manifested in our body. For we who live are always delivered to death for Jesus' sake, that the life of Jesus also may be manifested in our mortal flesh.

2 Corinthians 4:8–11

For our light affliction, which is but for a moment, is working for us a far more exceeding and eternal weight of glory, while we do not look at the things which are seen, but at the things which are not seen. For the things which are seen are temporary, but the things which are not seen are eternal.

2 Corinthians 4:17–18

Therefore do not cast away your confidence, which has great reward. For you have need of endurance, so that after you have done the will of God, you may receive the promise.

Hebrews 10:35–36

Through the LORD's mercies we are not
    consumed,
Because His compassions fail not.
They are new every morning;
Great is Your faithfulness.
"The LORD is my portion," says my soul,
"Therefore I hope in Him!"
The LORD is good to those who wait
    for Him,
To the soul who seeks Him.
Lamentations 3:22–25

For we know that if our earthly house, this
tent, is destroyed, we have a building from God, a
house not made with hands, eternal in the heavens.
2 Corinthians 5:1

I would have lost heart, unless I had believed
That I would see the goodness of the LORD
In the land of the living.
Wait on the LORD;
Be of good courage,
And He shall strengthen your heart;
Wait, I say, on the LORD!
Psalm 27:13–14

This hope we have as an anchor of the soul,
both sure and steadfast, and which enters the
Presence behind the veil.

Hebrews 6:19

I wait for the LORD, my soul waits,
And in His word I do hope.
My soul waits for the Lord
More than those who watch for the morning—
Yes, more than those who watch for
the morning.

Psalm 130:5–6

Every morning He brings His justice to light;
He never fails.

Zephaniah 3:5

Let us hold fast the confession of our hope
without wavering, for He who promised is faithful.

Hebrews 10:23

Rest in His Peace

For in the time of trouble
He shall hide me in His pavilion;
In the secret place of His tabernacle
He shall hide me;
He shall set me high upon a rock.

Psalm 27:5

Give us help from trouble,
For the help of man is useless.
Through God we will do valiantly,
For it is He who shall tread down our enemies.

Psalm 60:11–12

All your children shall be taught by
the LORD,
And great shall be the peace of your children.
In righteousness you shall be established;
You shall be far from oppression, for
you shall not fear;
And from terror, for it shall not come
near you.

Isaiah 54:13–14

Come to Me, all you who labor . . . and I will
give you rest.

Matthew 11:28

The LORD will guide you continually,
And satisfy your soul in drought,
And strengthen your bones;
You shall be like a watered garden,
And like a spring of water, whose waters
    do not fail.

Isaiah 58:11

The Spirit of the LORD God is upon Me,
Because the LORD has anointed Me
To preach good tidings to the poor;
He has sent Me to heal the brokenhearted,
To proclaim liberty to the captives,
And the opening of the prison to those
    who are bound.

Isaiah 61:1

When my father and my mother forsake me,
Then the LORD will take care of me.
I would have lost heart, unless I had believed
That I would see the goodness of the LORD
In the land of the living.
Wait on the LORD;
Be of good courage,
And He shall strengthen your heart;
Wait, I say, on the LORD!

Psalm 27:10, 13, 14

Let, I pray, Your merciful kindness be for
     my comfort,
According to Your word to Your servant.
Let Your tender mercies come to me, that
     I may live;
For Your law is my delight.

Psalm 119:76–77

Let the words of my mouth and the
     meditation of my heart
Be acceptable in Your sight,
O LORD, my strength and my Redeemer.

Psalm 19:14

Anxiety in the heart . . . causes depression,
but a good word makes it glad.

Proverbs 12:25

Stand Strong in Faith

You, beloved, building yourselves up on your most holy faith, praying in the Holy Spirit, keep yourselves in the love of God, looking for the mercy of our Lord Jesus Christ unto eternal life.

Jude 20–21

Be anxious for nothing, but in everything by prayer and supplication, with thanksgiving, let your requests be made known to God; and the peace of God, which surpasses all understanding, will guard your hearts and minds through Christ Jesus.

Philippians 4:6–7

Therefore, having been justified by faith, we have peace with God through our Lord Jesus Christ, through whom also we have access by faith into this grace in which we stand, and rejoice in hope of the glory of God.

Romans 5:1–2

The Lord is faithful, who will establish you and guard you from the evil one.

2 Thessalonians 3:3

My soul, wait silently for God alone,
For my expectation is from Him.
He only is my rock and my salvation;
He is my defense;
I shall not be moved.
In God is my salvation and my glory;
The rock of my strength,
And my refuge, is in God.

Psalm 62:5–7

Without faith it is impossible to please Him, for he who comes to God must believe that He is, and that He is a rewarder of those who diligently seek Him.

Hebrews 11:6

As Moses lifted up the serpent in the wilderness, even so must the Son of Man be lifted up, that whoever believes in Him should not perish but have eternal life.

John 3:14–15

Now faith is the substance of things hoped for, the evidence of things not seen. For by it the elders obtained a good testimony.

By faith we understand that the worlds were framed by the word of God, so that the things which are seen were not made of things which are visible.

Hebrews 11:1–3

Claim His Victory

He has put a new song in my mouth—
Praise to our God;
Many will see it and fear,
And will trust in the LORD.

Psalm 40:3

The LORD is near to those who have a
        broken heart,
And saves such as have a contrite spirit.
Many are the afflictions of the righteous,
But the LORD delivers him out of them all.
Psalm 34:18–19

The Spirit Himself bears witness with our
spirit that we are children of God, and if children,
then heirs—heirs of God and joint heirs with
Christ, if indeed we suffer with Him, that we may
also be glorified together.

For I consider that the sufferings of this present time are not worthy to be compared with the
glory which shall be revealed in us.

Romans 8:16–18

All that the Father gives Me will come to Me,
and the one who comes to Me I will by no means
cast out.

John 6:37

The earth is the LORD's, and all its fullness,
The world and those who dwell therein.
For He has founded it upon the seas,
And established it upon the waters.
Who may ascend into the hill of the LORD?
Or who may stand in His holy place?
He who has clean hands and a pure heart,
Who has not lifted up his soul to an idol,
Nor sworn deceitfully.
He shall receive blessing from the LORD,
And righteousness from the God of his
    salvation.
This is Jacob, the generation of those
    who seek Him,
Who seek Your face.
Lift up your heads, O you gates!
And be lifted up, you everlasting doors!
And the King of glory shall come in.
Who is this King of glory?
The LORD strong and mighty,
The LORD mighty in battle.
Lift up your heads, O you gates!
Lift up, you everlasting doors!
And the King of glory shall come in.
Who is this King of glory?
The LORD of hosts,
He is the King of glory.

Psalm 24:1–10

Great is the LORD, and greatly to be praised
In the city of our God,
In His holy mountain.

Psalm 48:1

The LORD is your keeper;
The LORD is your shade at your right hand.
The sun shall not strike you by day,
Nor the moon by night.
The LORD shall preserve you from all evil;
He shall preserve your soul.
The LORD shall preserve your going out
        and your coming in
From this time forth, and even forevermore.

Psalm 121:5–8

For God is the King of all the earth;
Sing praises with understanding.
God reigns over the nations;
God sits on His holy throne.
The princes of the people have gathered
        together,
The people of the God of Abraham.
For the shields of the earth belong to God;
He is greatly exalted.

Psalm 47:7–9

God Comforts Women as They Learn to . . .

Handle Spiritual Trials

Beloved, do not forget this one thing, that with the Lord one day is as a thousand years, and a thousand years as one day. The Lord is not slack concerning His promise, as some count slackness, but is longsuffering toward us, not willing that any should perish but that all should come to repentance.

2 Peter 3:8–9

Cast your burden on the LORD,
And He shall sustain you;
He shall never permit the righteous to
be moved.

Psalm 55:22

Blessed is the man who endures temptation; for when he has been approved, he will receive the crown of life which the Lord has promised to those who love Him.

For if anyone is a hearer of the word and not a doer, he is like a man observing his natural face in a mirror; for he observes himself, goes away, and immediately forgets what kind of man he was.

James 1:12, 23–24

But He knows the way that I take;
When He has tested me, I shall come forth
    as gold.
My foot has held fast to His steps;
I have kept His way and not turned aside.

Job 23:10–11

Why are you cast down, O my soul?
And why are you disquieted within me?
Hope in God;
For I shall yet praise Him,
The help of my countenance and my God.

Psalm 43:5

Beloved, do not think it strange concerning the fiery trial which is to try you, as though some strange thing happened to you; but rejoice to the extent that you partake of Christ's sufferings, that when His glory is revealed, you may also be glad with exceeding joy.

Yet if anyone suffers as a Christian, let him not be ashamed, but let him glorify God in this matter.

1 Peter 4:12–13, 16

I command you today to love the LORD your God, to walk in His ways, and to keep His commandments.

Deuteronomy 30:16

Hear me, O LORD, for Your lovingkindness
    is good;
Turn to me according to the multitude of
    Your tender mercies.
And do not hide Your face from Your servant,
For I am in trouble;
Hear me speedily.
Draw near to my soul, and redeem it;
Deliver me because of my enemies.

Psalm 69:16–18

He who covers his sins will not prosper,
But whoever confesses and forsakes them
    will have mercy.

Proverbs 28:13

Blessed are those who keep His testimonies,
who seek Him with the whole heart.

Psalm 119:2

Be ye doers of the word, and not hearers only,
deceiving yourselves.

James 1:22

Confront Serious Illness

Heal me, O LORD, and I shall be healed;
Save me, and I shall be saved,
For You are my praise.

Jeremiah 17:14

I said, "This is my anguish;
But I will remember the years of the
    right hand of the Most High."
I will remember the works of the LORD;
Surely I will remember Your wonders of old.
I will also meditate on all Your work,
And talk of Your deeds.
Your way, O God, is in the sanctuary;
Who is so great a God as our God?
You are the God who does wonders;
You have declared Your strength among
    the peoples.

Psalm 77:10–14

For this is God,
Our God forever and ever;
He will be our guide
Even to death.

Psalm 48:14

God will redeem my soul from the power
of the grave,
For He shall receive me.

Psalm 49:15

Yea, though I walk through the valley of the
shadow of death,
I will fear no evil;
For You are with me;
Your rod and Your staff, they comfort me.

Psalm 23:4

For we know that if our earthly house, this
tent, is destroyed, we have a building from God, a
house not made with hands, eternal in the heavens.

2 Corinthians 5:1

While I live I will praise the LORD;
I will sing praises to my God while I have my
being.

Psalm 146:2

Before I was afflicted I went astray,
But now I keep Your word.
You are good, and do good;
Teach me Your statutes.

Psalm 119:67–68

Handle Financial Problems 🌿

The Lord said, "Who then is that faithful and wise steward, whom his master will make ruler over his household, to give them their portion of food in due season? Blessed is that servant whom his master will find so doing when he comes. Truly, I say to you that he will make him ruler over all that he has."

Luke 12:42–44

Pray for the peace of Jerusalem:
May they prosper who love you.

Psalm 122:6

When He had fasted forty days and forty nights, afterward He was hungry. Now when the tempter came to Him, he said, "If You are the Son of God, command that these stones become bread."

But He answered and said, "It is written, 'Man shall not live by bread alone, but by every word that proceeds from the mouth of God.'"

Matthew 4:2–4

My God shall supply all your need according to His riches in glory by Christ Jesus.

Philippians 4:19

Listen, my beloved brethren: Has God not chosen the poor of this world to be rich in faith and heirs of the kingdom which He promised to those who love Him?

James 2:5

He who trusts in his riches will fall,
But the righteous will flourish like foliage.

Proverbs 11:28

Then He said to His disciples, "Therefore I say to you, do not worry about your life, what you will eat; nor about the body, what you will put on. Life is more than food, and the body is more than clothing. Consider the ravens, for they neither sow nor reap, which have neither storehouse nor barn; and God feeds them. Of how much more value are you than the birds?"

Luke 12:22–24

Poverty and shame will come to him who disdains correction,
But he who regards a rebuke will be honored.

Proverbs 13:18

Face the Years Ahead 🌿

For now we see in a mirror, dimly, but then face to face. Now I know in part, but then I shall know just as I also am known.

1 Corinthians 13:12

The righteous shall flourish like a palm tree,
He shall grow like a cedar in Lebanon.
Those who are planted in the house of the
      LORD
Shall flourish in the courts of our God.
They shall still bear fruit in old age;
They shall be fresh and flourishing,
To declare that the LORD is upright;
He is my rock, and there is no
      unrighteousness in Him.

Psalm 92:12–15

For none of us lives to himself, and no one dies to himself. For if we live, we live to the Lord; and if we die, we die to the Lord. Therefore, whether we live or die, we are the Lord's.

Romans 14:7–8

The fear of the LORD prolongs days,
But the years of the wicked will be shortened.

Proverbs 10:27

The days of our lives are seventy years;
And if by reason of strength they are
      eighty years,
Yet their boast is only labor and sorrow;
For it is soon cut off, and we fly away.
So teach us to number our days,
That we may gain a heart of wisdom.
Oh, satisfy us early with Your mercy,
That we may rejoice and be glad all our days!

Psalm 90:10, 12, 14

Older men be sober, reverent, temperate, sound in faith, in love, in patience; the older women likewise, that they be reverent in behavior, not slanderers, not given to much wine, teachers of good things— that they admonish the young women to love their husbands, to love their children.

Titus 2:2–4

But as for me, I trust in You, O LORD;
I say, "You are my God."
My times are in Your hand;
Deliver me from the hand of my enemies,
And from those who persecute me.

Psalm 31:14–15

For I know that my Redeemer lives,
And He shall stand at last on the earth;
And after my skin is destroyed, this I know,
That in my flesh I shall see God.

Job 19:25–26

Call on God's Divine Protection

I will both lie down in peace, and sleep;
For You alone, O LORD, make me dwell
in safety.

Psalm 4:8

The angel of the LORD encamps all around
those who fear Him,
And delivers them.

Psalm 34:7

He who dwells in the secret place of the
Most High
Shall abide under the shadow of the
Almighty.
I will say of the LORD, "He is my refuge and
my fortress;
My God, in Him I will trust."

Psalm 91:1–2

So shall they fear
The name of the LORD from the west,
And His glory from the rising of the sun;
When the enemy comes in like a flood,
The Spirit of the LORD will lift up a standard
against him.

Isaiah 59:19

The LORD is my light and my salvation;
Whom shall I fear?
The LORD is the strength of my life;
Of whom shall I be afraid?
For in the time of trouble
He shall hide me in His pavilion;
In the secret place of His tabernacle
He shall hide me;
He shall set me high upon a rock.

Psalm 27:1, 5

Are not two sparrows sold for a copper coin? And not one of them falls to the ground apart from your Father's will. But the very hairs of your head are all numbered. Do not fear therefore; you are of more value than many sparrows.

Matthew 10:29–31

The eternal God is your refuge,
And underneath are the everlasting arms;
He will thrust out the enemy from
        before you,
And will say, "Destroy!"

Deuteronomy 33:27

Whoever listens to me will dwell safely,
And will be secure, without fear of evil.

Proverbs 1:33

Be Content

"For the mountains shall depart
 And the hills be removed,
 But My kindness shall not depart from you,
 Nor shall My covenant of peace be
   removed,"
 Says the LORD, who has mercy on you.
"All your children shall be taught by the
   LORD,
 And great shall be the peace of your children.
 No weapon formed against you shall prosper,
 And every tongue which rises against you in
   judgment
 You shall condemn.
 This is the heritage of the servants of the
   LORD,
 And their righteousness is from Me,"
 Says the LORD.

Isaiah 54:10, 13, 17

Not that I speak in regard to need, for I have learned in whatever state I am, to be content: I know how to be abased, and I know how to abound. Everywhere and in all things I have learned both to be full and to be hungry, both to abound and to suffer need.

Philippians 4:11–12

There is therefore now no condemnation to those who are in Christ Jesus, who do not walk according to the flesh, but according to the Spirit. For the law of the Spirit of life in Christ Jesus has made me free from the law of sin and death.

For those who live according to the flesh set their minds on the things of the flesh, but those who live according to the Spirit, the things of the Spirit. For to be carnally minded is death, but to be spiritually minded is life and peace.

Romans 8:1–2, 5–6

Now godliness with contentment is great gain. For we brought nothing into this world, and it is certain we can carry nothing out. And having food and clothing, with these we shall be content.

1 Timothy 6:6–8

The LORD is my shepherd;
I shall not want.

Psalm 23:1

The LORD will guide you continually,
And satisfy your soul in drought,
And strengthen your bones;
You shall be like a watered garden,
And like a spring of water, whose waters
    do not fail.

Isaiah 58:11

Not that we are sufficient of ourselves to think of anything as being from ourselves, but our sufficiency is from God.

2 Corinthians 3:5

The LORD is your keeper;
The LORD is your shade at your right hand.
The LORD shall preserve your going out
     and your coming in
From this time forth, and even forevermore.
Psalm 121:5, 8

Eye has not seen, nor ear heard . . . the things which God has prepared for those who love Him.
1 Corinthians 2:9

You are complete in Him, who is the head of all principality and power.

Colossians 2:10

God Gives Freely to Women . . .

Hope for Eternal Life

Sing to the LORD with thanksgiving;
Sing praises on the harp to our God,
Who covers the heavens with clouds,
Who prepares rain for the earth,
Who makes grass to grow on the mountains.
He gives to the beast its food,
And to the young ravens that cry.
He does not delight in the strength of the
    horse;
He takes no pleasure in the legs of a man.
The LORD takes pleasure in those who fear
    Him,
In those who hope in His mercy.
Praise the LORD, O Jerusalem!
Praise your God, O Zion!
For He has strengthened the bars of your
    gates;
He has blessed your children within you.

Psalm 147:7–13

If then you were raised with Christ, seek those things which are above, where Christ is, sitting at the right hand of God. Set your mind on things above, not on things on the earth. For you died, and your life is hidden with Christ in God. When Christ who is our life appears, then you also will appear with Him in glory.

Colossians 3:1–4

Let us who are of the day be sober, putting on the breastplate of faith and love, and as a helmet the hope of salvation. For God did not appoint us to wrath, but to obtain salvation through our Lord Jesus Christ, who died for us, that whether we wake or sleep, we should live together with Him.

Therefore comfort each other and edify one another, just as you also are doing.

1 Thessalonians 5:8–11

God, who is rich in mercy, because of His great love with which He loved us, even when we were dead in trespasses, made us alive together with Christ (by grace you have been saved), and raised us up together, and made us sit together in the heavenly places in Christ Jesus, that in the ages to come He might show the exceeding riches of His grace in His kindness toward us in Christ Jesus.

Ephesians 2:4–7

I have fought the good fight, I have finished the race, I have kept the faith. Finally, there is laid up for me the crown of righteousness, which the Lord, the righteous Judge, will give to me on that Day, and not to me only but also to all who have loved His appearing.

2 Timothy 4:7–8

Knowing that a man is not justified by the works of the law but by faith in Jesus Christ, even we have believed in Christ Jesus, that we might be justified by faith in Christ and not by the works of the law; for by the works of the law no flesh shall be justified.

I have been crucified with Christ; it is no longer I who live, but Christ lives in me; and the life which I now live in the flesh I live by faith in the Son of God, who loved me and gave Himself for me.

Galatians 2:16, 20

For as many as are led by the Spirit of God, these are sons of God. For you did not receive the spirit of bondage again to fear, but you received the Spirit of adoption by whom we cry out, "Abba, Father." The Spirit Himself bears witness with our spirit that we are children of God, and if children, then heirs—heirs of God and joint heirs with Christ, if indeed we suffer with Him, that we may also be glorified together.

For I consider that the sufferings of this present time are not worthy to be compared with the glory which shall be revealed in us.

For we were saved in this hope, but hope that is seen is not hope; for why does one still hope for what he sees? But if we hope for what we do not see, we eagerly wait for it with perseverance.

Romans 8:14–18, 24–25

Blessed be the God and Father of our Lord Jesus Christ, who according to His abundant mercy has begotten us again to a living hope through the resurrection of Jesus Christ from the dead, to an inheritance incorruptible and undefiled and that does not fade away, reserved in heaven for you, who are kept by the power of God through faith for salvation ready to be revealed in the last time.

In this you greatly rejoice, though now for a little while, if need be, you have been grieved by various trials, that the genuineness of your faith, being much more precious than gold that perishes, though it is tested by fire, may be found to praise, honor, and glory at the revelation of Jesus Christ, whom having not seen you love. Though now you do not see Him, yet believing, you rejoice with joy inexpressible and full of glory, receiving the end of your faith—the salvation of your souls.

1 Peter 1:3–9

Because of the hope which is laid up for you in heaven, of which you heard before in the word of the truth of the gospel, which has come to you, as it has also in all the world, and is bringing forth fruit, as it is also among you since the day you heard and knew the grace of God in truth.

Colossians 1:5–6

Wisdom for Daily Living

My son, pay attention to my wisdom;
Lend your ear to my understanding,
That you may preserve discretion,
And your lips may keep knowledge.

Proverbs 5:1–2

The fear of the LORD is the beginning of
    wisdom;
A good understanding have all those who do
    His commandments.
His praise endures forever.

Psalm 111:10

The days of our lives are seventy years;
And if by reason of strength they are
    eighty years,
Yet their boast is only labor and sorrow;
For it is soon cut off, and we fly away.
Who knows the power of Your anger?
For as the fear of You, so is Your wrath.
So teach us to number our days,
That we may gain a heart of wisdom.

Psalm 90:10–12

How much better to get wisdom than gold!
And to get understanding is to be
    chosen rather than silver.

Proverbs 16:16

A wise man fears and departs from evil,
But a fool rages and is self-confident.

Proverbs 14:16

Happy is the man who finds wisdom,
And the man who gains understanding;
For her proceeds are better than the profits
    of silver,
And her gain than fine gold.
She is more precious than rubies,
And all the things you may desire cannot
    compare with her.
Length of days is in her right hand,
In her left hand riches and honor.
Her ways are ways of pleasantness,
And all her paths are peace.
She is a tree of life to those who take hold
    of her,
And happy are all who retain her.
The LORD by wisdom founded the earth;
By understanding He established the heavens;
By His knowledge the depths were
    broken up,
And clouds drop down the dew.
My son, let them not depart from
    your eyes—
Keep sound wisdom and discretion;
So they will be life to your soul
And grace to your neck.

Proverbs 3:13–22

If any of you lacks wisdom, let him ask of God, who gives to all liberally and without reproach, and it will be given to him. But let him ask in faith, with no doubting, for he who doubts is like a wave of the sea driven and tossed by the wind.

James 1:5–6

Get wisdom! Get understanding!
Do not forget, nor turn away from the
    words of my mouth.
Do not forsake her, and she will
    preserve you;
Love her, and she will keep you.
Wisdom is the principal thing;
Therefore get wisdom.
And in all your getting, get understanding.
Exalt her, and she will promote you;
She will bring you honor, when you
    embrace her.
She will place on your head an ornament
    of grace;
A crown of glory she will deliver to you.
Hear, my son, and receive my sayings,
And the years of your life will be many.
I have taught you in the way of wisdom;
I have led you in right paths.

Proverbs 4:5–11

My son, keep my words,
And treasure my commands within you.
Keep my commands and live,
And my law as the apple of your eye.
Bind them on your fingers;
Write them on the tablet of your heart.
Say to wisdom, "You are my sister,"
And call understanding your nearest kin,
That they may keep you from the immoral
    woman,
From the seductress who flatters with her
    words.

Proverbs 7:1–5

The fear of the LORD is the beginning of
    wisdom,
And the knowledge of the Holy One is
    understanding.
For by me your days will be multiplied,
And years of life will be added to you.
If you are wise, you are wise for yourself,
And if you scoff, you will bear it alone.

Proverbs 9:10–12

The wisdom that is from above is first pure,
then peaceable, gentle, willing to yield, full of
mercy and good fruits, without partiality and
without hypocrisy.

James 3:17

Victory Over Sin

Therefore, if anyone is in Christ, he is a new creation; old things have passed away; behold, all things have become new. Now all things are of God, who has reconciled us to Himself through Jesus Christ, and has given us the ministry of reconciliation, that is, that God was in Christ reconciling the world to Himself, not imputing their trespasses to them, and has committed to us the word of reconciliation.

Now then, we are ambassadors for Christ, as though God were pleading through us: we implore you on Christ's behalf, be reconciled to God. For He made Him who knew no sin to be sin for us, that we might become the righteousness of God in Him.

2 Corinthians 5:17–21

O God, You know my foolishness;
And my sins are not hidden from You.

Psalm 69:5

For as many as are of the works of the law are under the curse; for it is written, "Cursed is everyone who does not continue in all things which are written in the book of the law, to do them." But that no one is justified by the law in the sight of God is evident, for the just shall live by faith.

Galatians 3:10–11

Stand fast therefore in the liberty by which Christ has made us free, and do not be entangled again with a yoke of bondage.

Galatians 5:1

This is the message which we have heard from Him and declare to you, that God is light and in Him is no darkness at all. If we say that we have fellowship with Him, and walk in darkness, we lie and do not practice the truth. But if we walk in the light as He is in the light, we have fellowship with one another, and the blood of Jesus Christ His Son cleanses us from all sin.

If we say that we have no sin, we deceive ourselves, and the truth is not in us. If we confess our sins, He is faithful and just to forgive us our sins and to cleanse us from all unrighteousness. If we say that we have not sinned, we make Him a liar, and His word is not in us.

1 John 1:5–10

It is no longer I who live, but Christ lives in me.
Galatians 2:20

Create in me a clean heart, O God, and renew a steadfast spirit within me.

Psalm 51:10

"Wash yourselves, make yourselves clean;
Put away the evil of your doings from
     before My eyes.
Cease to do evil,
Learn to do good;
Seek justice,
Rebuke the oppressor;
Defend the fatherless,
Plead for the widow.
Come now, and let us reason together,"
Says the LORD,
"Though your sins are like scarlet,
They shall be as white as snow;
Though they are red like crimson,
They shall be as wool.
If you are willing and obedient,
You shall eat the good of the land."

Isaiah 1:16–19

You know that He was manifested to take away our sins, and in Him there is no sin. Whoever abides in Him does not sin. Whoever sins has neither seen Him nor known Him. Little children, let no one deceive you. He who practices righteousness is righteous, just as He is righteous.

1 John 3:5–7

I have taught you in the way of wisdom; I have led you in right paths.

Proverbs 4:11

Therefore, since we have this ministry, as we have received mercy, we do not lose heart. But we have renounced the hidden things of shame, not walking in craftiness nor handling the word of God deceitfully, but by manifestation of the truth commending ourselves to every man's conscience in the sight of God. But even if our gospel is veiled, it is veiled to those who are perishing, whose minds the god of this age has blinded, who do not believe, lest the light of the gospel of the glory of Christ, who is the image of God, should shine on them. For we do not preach ourselves, but Christ Jesus the Lord, and ourselves your bondservants for Jesus' sake. For it is the God who commanded light to shine out of darkness, who has shone in our hearts to give the light of the knowledge of the glory of God in the face of Jesus Christ.

2 Corinthians 4:1–6

Comfort in Troubled Times

The LORD builds up Jerusalem;
He gathers together the outcasts of Israel.
He heals the brokenhearted
And binds up their wounds.
Great is our Lord, and mighty in power;
His understanding is infinite.
The LORD lifts up the humble;
He casts the wicked down to the ground.
For He has strengthened the bars of your
      gates;
He has blessed your children within you.
He makes peace in your borders,
And fills you with the finest wheat.
Psalm 147:2–3, 5–6, 13–14

Peace I leave with you, My peace I give to
you; not as the world gives do I give to you. Let
not your heart be troubled, neither let it be afraid.
John 14:27

Turn Yourself to me, and have mercy on me,
For I am desolate and afflicted.
The troubles of my heart have enlarged;
Bring me out of my distresses!
Look on my affliction and my pain,
And forgive all my sins.
Psalm 25:16–18

Casting all your care upon Him, for He cares for you.

Be sober, be vigilant; because your adversary the devil walks about like a roaring lion, seeking whom he may devour. Resist him, steadfast in the faith, knowing that the same sufferings are experienced by your brotherhood in the world. But may the God of all grace, who called us to His eternal glory by Christ Jesus, after you have suffered a while, perfect, establish, strengthen, and settle you. To Him be the glory and the dominion forever and ever. Amen.

1 Peter 5:7–11

A horse is a vain hope for safety;
Neither shall it deliver any by its
    great strength.
Behold, the eye of the LORD is on those
    who fear Him,
On those who hope in His mercy,
To deliver their soul from death,
And to keep them alive in famine.
Our soul waits for the LORD;
He is our help and our shield.
For our heart shall rejoice in Him,
Because we have trusted in His holy name.
Let Your mercy, O LORD, be upon us,
Just as we hope in You.

Psalm 33:17–22

For none of us lives to himself, and no one dies to himself.

Romans 14:7

I will bless the LORD at all times;
His praise shall continually be in my mouth.
My soul shall make its boast in the LORD;
The humble shall hear of it and be glad.
Oh, magnify the LORD with me,
And let us exalt His name together.
I sought the LORD, and He heard me,
And delivered me from all my fears.
They looked to Him and were radiant,
And their faces were not ashamed.
This poor man cried out, and the
    LORD heard him,
And saved him out of all his troubles.
The angel of the LORD encamps all
    around those who fear Him,
And delivers them.
Oh, taste and see that the LORD is good;
Blessed is the man who trusts in Him!

Psalm 34:1–8

I will be glad and rejoice in Your mercy,
For You have considered my trouble;
You have known my soul in adversities.

Psalm 31:7

Power to Defeat Fear

Yet in all these things we are more than conquerors through Him who loved us. For I am persuaded that neither death nor life, nor angels nor principalities nor powers, nor things present nor things to come, nor height nor depth, nor any other created thing, shall be able to separate us from the love of God which is in Christ Jesus our Lord.

Romans 8:37–39

For You will light my lamp;
The LORD my God will enlighten my
     darkness.
For by You I can run against a troop,
By my God I can leap over a wall.
As for God, His way is perfect;
The word of the LORD is proven;
He is a shield to all who trust in Him.

Psalm 18:28–30

Then Jesus spoke to them again, saying, "I am the light of the world. He who follows Me shall not walk in darkness, but have the light of life."

John 8:12

The LORD is my light and my salvation;
Whom shall I fear?
The LORD is the strength of my life;
Of whom shall I be afraid?
When the wicked came against me
To eat up my flesh,
My enemies and foes,
They stumbled and fell.
Though an army may encamp against me,
My heart shall not fear;
Though war may rise against me,
In this I will be confident.
One thing I have desired of the LORD,
That will I seek:
That I may dwell in the house of the LORD
All the days of my life,
To behold the beauty of the LORD,
And to inquire in His temple.
For in the time of trouble
He shall hide me in His pavilion;
In the secret place of His tabernacle
He shall hide me;
He shall set me high upon a rock.
And now my head shall be lifted up above
      my enemies all around me;
Therefore I will offer sacrifices of joy in His
      tabernacle;
I will sing, yes, I will sing praises to the LORD.
Hear, O LORD, when I cry with my voice!
Have mercy also upon me, and answer me.

Psalm 27:1–7

Do not be afraid of sudden terror,
Nor of trouble from the wicked when
  it comes;
For the LORD will be your confidence,
And will keep your foot from being caught.

Proverbs 3:25–26

Delight yourself also in the LORD,
And He shall give you the desires of your
  heart.
Commit your way to the LORD,
Trust also in Him,
And He shall bring it to pass.
He shall bring forth your righteousness
  as the light,
And your justice as the noonday.

Psalm 37:4–6

I will love You, O LORD, my strength.
The LORD is my rock and my fortress and
  my deliverer;
My God, my strength, in whom I will trust;
My shield and the horn of my salvation, my
  stronghold.
I will call upon the LORD, who is worthy to
  be praised;
So shall I be saved from my enemies.

Psalm 18:1–3

The LORD your God himself crosses over before you . . . He will be with you, He will not leave you nor forsake you.

Deuteronomy 31:3, 8

Your ears shall hear a voice behind you saying, "This is the way; walk in it."

Isaiah 30:21

Let us therefore come boldly to the throne of grace, that we may obtain mercy and find grace to help in time of need.

Hebrews 4:16

Courage to Be Women
of Integrity

Blessed is the man
Who walks not in the counsel of the ungodly,
Nor stands in the path of sinners,
Nor sits in the seat of the scornful;
But his delight is in the law of the LORD,
And in His law he meditates day and night.
He shall be like a tree
Planted by the rivers of water,
That brings forth its fruit in its season,
Whose leaf also shall not wither;
And whatever he does shall prosper.
The ungodly are not so,
But are like the chaff which the wind drives
     away.
Therefore the ungodly shall not stand in
     the judgment,
Nor sinners in the congregation of the righteous.
For the LORD knows the way of the
     righteous,
But the way of the ungodly shall perish.

Psalm 1:1–6

The LORD shall judge the peoples;
Judge me, O LORD, according to my
     righteousness,
And according to my integrity within me.

Psalm 7:8

The righteous man walks in his integrity;
His children are blessed after him.

Proverbs 20:7

I will behave wisely in a perfect way.
Oh, when will You come to me?
I will walk within my house with a
perfect heart.
I will set nothing wicked before my eyes;
I hate the work of those who fall away;
It shall not cling to me.
A perverse heart shall depart from me;
I will not know wickedness.
Whoever secretly slanders his neighbor,
Him I will destroy;
The one who has a haughty look and a
proud heart,
Him I will not endure.
My eyes shall be on the faithful of the land,
That they may dwell with me;
He who walks in a perfect way,
He shall serve me.
He who works deceit shall not dwell within
my house;
He who tells lies shall not continue in my
presence.
Early I will destroy all the wicked of the land,
That I may cut off all the evildoers from the
city of the LORD.

Psalm 101:2–8

He who speaks truth declares righteousness,
But a false witness, deceit.
There is one who speaks like the piercings
    of a sword,
But the tongue of the wise promotes health.
The truthful lip shall be established forever,
But a lying tongue is but for a moment.
Proverbs 12:17–19

A good man deals graciously and lends;
He will guide his affairs with discretion.
Surely he will never be shaken;
The righteous will be in everlasting
    remembrance.
He will not be afraid of evil tidings;
His heart is steadfast, trusting in the LORD.
Psalm 112:5–7

The LORD shall judge the peoples;
Judge me, O LORD, according to my
    righteousness,
And according to my integrity within me.
Psalm 7:8

If I have walked with falsehood,
Or if my foot has hastened to deceit,
Let me be weighed on honest scales,
That God may know my integrity.
Job 31:5–6

Far be it from me
That I should say you are right;
Till I die I will not put away my integrity
from me.
My righteousness I hold fast, and will not let
it go;
My heart shall not reproach me as long as
I live.

Job 27:5–6

Blessed are the undefiled in the way,
Who walk in the law of the LORD!
Blessed are those who keep His testimonies,
Who seek Him with the whole heart!
They also do no iniquity;
They walk in His ways.
You have commanded us
To keep Your precepts diligently.
Oh, that my ways were directed
To keep Your statutes!
Then I would not be ashamed,
When I look into all Your commandments.
I will praise You with uprightness of heart,
When I learn Your righteous judgments.
I will keep Your statutes;
Oh, do not forsake me utterly!

Psalm 119:1–8

God Helps Women to Grow by . . .

Recognizing Evil

There is a way that seems right to a man,
But its end is the way of death.

Proverbs 14:12

Beware of false prophets, who come to you in sheep's clothing, but inwardly they are ravenous wolves. You will know them by their fruits. Do men gather grapes from thornbushes or figs from thistles?

Matthew 7:15–16

By this you know the Spirit of God: Every spirit that confesses that Jesus Christ has come in the flesh is of God, and every spirit that does not confess that Jesus Christ has come in the flesh is not of God. And this is the spirit of the Antichrist, which you have heard was coming, and is now already in the world.

1 John 4:2–3

For God is not the author of confusion but of peace, as in all the churches of the saints.

1 Corinthians 14:33

They profess to know God, but in works they deny Him, being abominable, disobedient, and disqualified for every good work.

Titus 1:16

For God has not given us a spirit of fear, but of power and of love and of a sound mind.

2 Timothy 1:7

For certain men have crept in unnoticed, who long ago were marked out for this condemnation, ungodly men, who turn the grace of our God into lewdness and deny the only Lord God and our Lord Jesus Christ.

Jude 4

For many deceivers have gone out into the world who do not confess Jesus Christ as coming in the flesh. This is a deceiver and an antichrist.

Whoever transgresses and does not abide in the doctrine of Christ does not have God. He who abides in the doctrine of Christ has both the Father and the Son. If anyone comes to you and does not bring this doctrine, do not receive him into your house nor greet him; for he who greets him shares in his evil deeds.

2 John 7, 9–11

Your word is a lamp to my feet and a light to my path.

Psalm 119:105

Controlling the Tongue

Let no corrupt word proceed out of your mouth, but what is good for necessary edification, that it may impart grace to the hearers.

Ephesians 4:29

As long as my breath is in me,
And the breath of God in my nostrils,
My lips will not speak wickedness,
Nor my tongue utter deceit.

Job 27:3–4

He who would love life
And see good days,
Let him refrain his tongue from evil,
And his lips from speaking deceit.

1 Peter 3:10

Do not be a witness against your
neighbor without cause,
For would you deceive with your lips?

Proverbs 24:28

Whoever guards his mouth and tongue
Keeps his soul from troubles.

Proverbs 21:23

A good man out of the good treasure of his heart brings forth good; and an evil man out of the evil treasure of his heart brings forth evil. For out of the abundance of the heart his mouth speaks.

Luke 6:45

A wholesome tongue is a tree of life,
But perverseness in it breaks the spirit.

Proverbs 15:4

If anyone among you thinks he is religious, and does not bridle his tongue but deceives his own heart, this one's religion is useless.

James 1:26

Whoever offers praise glorifies Me;
And to him who orders his conduct aright
I will show the salvation of God.

Psalm 50:23

Set a guard, O LORD, over my mouth;
Keep watch over the door of my lips.

Psalm 141:3

Dealing with Lust 🌿

Submit to God. Resist the devil and he will flee from you.

James 4:7

I say then: Walk in the Spirit, and you shall not fulfill the lust of the flesh. For the flesh lusts against the Spirit, and the Spirit against the flesh; and these are contrary to one another, so that you do not do the things that you wish.

Galatians 5:16–17

Each one is tempted when he is drawn away by his own desires and enticed. Then, when desire has conceived, it gives birth to sin; and sin, when it is full-grown, brings forth death.

Do not be deceived, my beloved brethren.

James 1:14–16

Then the Lord knows how to deliver the godly out of temptations and to reserve the unjust under punishment for the day of judgment.

2 Peter 2:9

A man with an evil eye hastens after riches,
And does not consider that poverty
    will come upon him.

Proverbs 28:22

The LORD is far from the wicked,
But He hears the prayer of the righteous.

Proverbs 15:29

For this you know, that no fornicator, unclean person, nor covetous man, who is an idolater, has any inheritance in the kingdom of Christ and God.

Therefore do not be partakers with them.

For you were once darkness, but now you are light in the Lord. Walk as children of light (for the fruit of the Spirit is in all goodness, righteousness, and truth).

And do not be drunk with wine, in which is dissipation; but be filled with the Spirit.

Ephesians 5:5, 7–9, 18

That you put off, concerning your former conduct, the old man which grows corrupt according to the deceitful lusts, and be renewed in the spirit of your mind, and that you put on the new man which was created according to God, in true righteousness and holiness.

Nor give place to the devil.

Ephesians 4:22–24, 27

Likewise you also, reckon yourselves to be dead indeed to sin, but alive to God in Christ Jesus our Lord.

Therefore do not let sin reign in your mortal body, that you should obey it in its lusts.

Romans 6:11–12

Overcoming Wordliness 🌼

Do not be conformed to this world, but be transformed by the renewing of your mind, that you may prove what is that good and acceptable and perfect will of God.

Romans 12:2

Have no fellowship with the unfruitful works of darkness, but rather expose them.

Ephesians 5:11

Then He said to them all, "If anyone desires to come after Me, let him deny himself, and take up his cross daily, and follow Me. For whoever desires to save his life will lose it, but whoever loses his life for My sake will save it. For what profit is it to a man if he gains the whole world, and is himself destroyed or lost?"

Luke 9:23–25

Do not love the world or the things in the world. If anyone loves the world, the love of the Father is not in him. For all that is in the world—the lust of the flesh, the lust of the eyes, and the pride of life—is not of the Father but is of the world. And the world is passing away, and the lust of it; but he who does the will of God abides forever.

1 John 2:15–17

We have renounced the hidden things of shame, not walking in craftiness nor handling the word of God deceitfully, but by manifestation of the truth commending ourselves to every man's conscience in the sight of God.

2 Corinthians 4:2

Set your mind on things above, not on things on the earth.

Do not lie to one another, since you have put off the old man with his deeds, and have put on the new man who is renewed in knowledge according to the image of Him who created him.

Colossians 3:2, 9–10

Teaching us that, denying ungodliness and worldly lusts, we should live soberly, righteously, and godly in the present age, looking for the blessed hope and glorious appearing of our great God and Savior Jesus Christ.

Titus 2:12–13

These things I have spoken to you, that in Me you may have peace. In the world you will have tribulation; but be of good cheer, I have overcome the world.

John 16:33

He said to them, "Take heed and beware of covetousness, for one's life does not consist in the abundance of the things he possesses."

Luke 12:15

Do not be unequally yoked together with unbelievers. For what fellowship has righteousness with lawlessness? And what communion has light with darkness?
"Come out from among them
And be separate, says the Lord.
Do not touch what is unclean,
And I will receive you."

2 Corinthians 6:14, 17

But you are a chosen generation, a royal priesthood, a holy nation, His own special people.

1 Peter 2:9

Putting Aside Pride

Yet it shall not be so among you; but whoever desires to become great among you, let him be your servant. And whoever desires to be first among you, let him be your slave.

Matthew 20:26–27

Likewise you younger people, submit yourselves to your elders. Yes, all of you be submissive to one another, and be clothed with humility, for
"God resists the proud,
But gives grace to the humble."
Therefore humble yourselves under the mighty hand of God, that He may exalt you in due time.

1 Peter 5:5–6

A man's pride will bring him low,
But the humble in spirit will retain honor.

Proverbs 29:23

By humility and the fear of the LORD
Are riches and honor and life.

Proverbs 22:4

Though the LORD is on high,
Yet He regards the lowly;
But the proud He knows from afar.

Psalm 138:6

The Pharisee stood and prayed thus with himself, "God, I thank You that I am not like other men—extortioners, unjust, adulterers, or even as this tax collector. I fast twice a week; I give tithes of all that I possess." And the tax collector, standing afar off, would not so much as raise his eyes to heaven, but beat his breast, saying, "God, be merciful to me a sinner!" I tell you, this man went down to his house justified rather than the other; for everyone who exalts himself will be humbled, and he who humbles himself will be exalted.

Luke 18:11–14

He who glories, let him glory in the LORD. For not he who commends himself is approved, but whom the Lord commends.

2 Corinthians 10:17–18

Pride goes before destruction,
And a haughty spirit before a fall.
Better to be of a humble spirit with the lowly,
Than to divide the spoil with the proud.
He who heeds the word wisely will
    find good,
And whoever trusts in the LORD, happy is he.

Proverbs 16:18–20

Submit to God. Resist the devil and he will flee from you.

Humble yourselves in the sight of the Lord, and He will lift you up.

James 4:7, 10

As the elect of God, holy and beloved, put on tender mercies, kindness, humility, meekness, longsuffering.

Colossians 3:12

Walk worthy of the calling with which you were called, with all lowliness and gentleness.

Ephesians 4:1

Rejoicing in the Lord 🌸

Let the word of Christ dwell in you richly in all wisdom, teaching and admonishing one another in psalms and hymns and spiritual songs, singing with grace in your hearts to the Lord.

Colossians 3:16

Then he said to them, "Go your way, eat the fat, drink the sweet, and send portions to those for whom nothing is prepared; for this day is holy to our LORD. Do not sorrow, for the joy of the LORD is your strength."

Nehemiah 8:10

Those who sow in tears
Shall reap in joy.
He who continually goes forth weeping,
Bearing seed for sowing,
Shall doubtless come again with rejoicing,
Bringing his sheaves with him.

Psalm 126:5–6

Restore to me the joy of Your salvation,
And uphold me by Your generous Spirit.
Then I will teach transgressors Your ways,
And sinners shall be converted to You.

Psalm 51:12–13

This is the day the LORD has made;
We will rejoice and be glad in it.

Psalm 118:24

His lord said to him, "Well done, good and faithful servant; you were faithful over a few things, I will make you ruler over many things. Enter into the joy of your lord."

Matthew 25:21

These things I have spoken to you, that My joy may remain in you, and that your joy may be full. This is My commandment, that you love one another as I have loved you.

John 15:11–12

You became followers of us and of the Lord, having received the word in much affliction, with joy of the Holy Spirit.

1 Thessalonians 1:6

My lips shall greatly rejoice when I sing to You, and my soul, which You have redeemed.

Psalm 71:23

God Rejoices with Women When They . . .

Join with Other Believers

You call me Teacher and Lord, and you say well, for so I am. If I then, your Lord and Teacher, have washed your feet, you also ought to wash one another's feet. For I have given you an example, that you should do as I have done to you. Most assuredly, I say to you, a servant is not greater than his master; nor is he who is sent greater than he who sent him. If you know these things, blessed are you if you do them.

John 13:13–17

God is faithful, by whom you were called into the fellowship of His Son, Jesus Christ our Lord.

Now I plead with you, brethren, by the name of our Lord Jesus Christ, that you all speak the same thing, and that there be no divisions among you, but that you be perfectly joined together in the same mind and in the same judgment.

1 Corinthians 1:9–10

He who says he is in the light, and hates his brother, is in darkness until now. He who loves his brother abides in the light, and there is no cause for stumbling in him. But he who hates his brother is in darkness and walks in darkness, and does not know where he is going, because the darkness has blinded his eyes.

1 John 2:9–11

God, who is rich in mercy, because of His great love with which He loved us, even when we were dead in trespasses, made us alive together with Christ (by grace you have been saved), and raised us up together, and made us sit together in the heavenly places in Christ Jesus.

Ephesians 2:4–6

Now John answered Him, saying, "Teacher, we saw someone who does not follow us casting out demons in Your name, and we forbade him because he does not follow us."

But Jesus said, "Do not forbid him, for no one who works a miracle in My name can soon afterward speak evil of Me. For he who is not against us is on our side. For whoever gives you a cup of water to drink in My name, because you belong to Christ, assuredly, I say to you, he will by no means lose his reward.

But whoever causes one of these little ones who believe in Me to stumble, it would be better for him if a millstone were hung around his neck, and he were thrown into the sea."

Mark 9:38–42

You are a chosen generation, a royal priesthood, a holy nation, His own special people, that you may proclaim the praises of Him who called you out of darkness into His marvelous light.

1 Peter 2:9

Now indeed there are many members, yet one body. And the eye cannot say to the hand, "I have no need of you"; nor again the head to the feet, "I have no need of you." No, much rather, those members of the body which seem to be weaker are necessary. And those members of the body which we think to be less honorable, on these we bestow greater honor; and our unpresentable parts have greater modesty, but our presentable parts have no need. But God composed the body, having given greater honor to that part which lacks it, that there should be no schism in the body, but that the members should have the same care for one another. And if one member suffers, all the members suffer with it; or if one member is honored, all the members rejoice with it.

Now you are the body of Christ, and members individually.

1 Corinthians 12:20–27

If we say that we have fellowship with Him, and walk in darkness, we lie and do not practice the truth. But if we walk in the light as He is in the light, we have fellowship with one another, and the blood of Jesus Christ His Son cleanses us from all sin.

1 John 1:6–7

Seek to Understand
God's Ways 🌸

Forsake foolishness and live,
And go in the way of understanding.
The fear of the LORD is the beginning of
    wisdom,
And the knowledge of the Holy One
    is understanding.

Proverbs 9:6, 10

How much better to get wisdom than gold!
And to get understanding is to be
    chosen rather than silver.
The highway of the upright is to depart
    from evil;
He who keeps his way preserves his soul.

Proverbs 16:16–17

Seek the LORD while He may be found,
Call upon Him while He is near.
"For My thoughts are not your thoughts,
Nor are your ways My ways," says the LORD.
For as the heavens are higher than the earth,
So are My ways higher than your ways,
And My thoughts than your thoughts.

Isaiah 55:6, 8–9

If any of you lacks wisdom, let him ask of God, who gives to all liberally and without reproach, and it will be given to him.

James 1:5

Make me understand the way of Your
    precepts;
So shall I meditate on Your wonderful works.
Give me understanding, and I shall
    keep Your law;
Indeed, I shall observe it with my
    whole heart.
Your hands have made me and fashioned me;
Give me understanding, that I may
    learn Your commandments.
You, through Your commandments,
    make me wiser than my enemies;
For they are ever with me.
Through Your precepts I get understanding;
Therefore I hate every false way.
Your word is a lamp to my feet
And a light to my path.
I am Your servant;
Give me understanding,
That I may know Your testimonies.
    Psalm 119:27, 34, 73, 98, 104–105, 125

But there is a spirit in man,
And the breath of the Almighty gives him
    understanding.

Job 32:8

Great is our Lord, and mighty in power;
His understanding is infinite.

Psalm 147:5

For the LORD gives wisdom;
From His mouth come knowledge
and understanding;
He stores up sound wisdom for the upright;
He is a shield to those who walk uprightly.

Proverbs 2:6–7

Lead me in Your truth and teach me, for You
are the God of my salvation.

Psalm 25:5

I applied my heart to know, to search and
seek out wisdom and the reason for things.

Ecclesiastes 7:25

Stand in Awe of the Lord 🌿

If you seek her as silver,
And search for her as for hidden treasures;
Then you will understand the fear of
the LORD,
And find the knowledge of God.

Proverbs 2:4–5

He does not delight in the strength of
the horse;
He takes no pleasure in the legs of a man.
The LORD takes pleasure in those who
fear Him,
In those who hope in His mercy.

Psalm 147:10–11

The fear of the LORD is the beginning
of knowledge,
But fools despise wisdom and instruction.

Proverbs 1:7

The fear of the LORD leads to life,
And he who has it will abide in satisfaction;
He will not be visited with evil.

Proverbs 19:23

In the fear of the LORD there is strong
    confidence,
And His children will have a place of refuge.
The fear of the LORD is a fountain of life,
To turn one away from the snares of death.
Proverbs 14:26–27

Then those who feared the LORD spoke
    to one another,
And the LORD listened and heard them;
So a book of remembrance was
    written before Him
For those who fear the LORD
And who meditate on His name.
"They shall be Mine," says the LORD
    of hosts,
"On the day that I make them My jewels.
And I will spare them
As a man spares his own son who
    serves him."
Malachi 3:16–17

Let us hear the conclusion of the whole matter:
Fear God and keep His commandments,
For this is man's all.
For God will bring every work into
    judgment,
Including every secret thing,
Whether good or evil.
Ecclesiastes 12:13–14

Praise the LORD!
Blessed is the man who fears the LORD,
Who delights greatly in His commandments.

Psalm 112:1

In mercy and truth
Atonement is provided for iniquity;
And by the fear of the LORD one
    departs from evil.

Proverbs 16:6

Who is the man that fears the LORD?
Him shall He teach in the way He chooses.
He himself shall dwell in prosperity,
And his descendants shall inherit the earth.
The secret of the LORD is with those who
    fear Him,
And He will show them His covenant.

Psalm 25:12–14

Behold, the fear of the Lord, that is wisdom,
And to depart from evil is understanding.

Job 28:28

Seek His Sovereignty

For the LORD is our Judge,
The LORD is our Lawgiver,
The LORD is our King;
He will save us.

Isaiah 33:22

Then Moses said to God, "Indeed, when I
come to the children of Israel and say to them,
'The God of your fathers has sent me to you,' and
they say to me, 'What is His name?' what shall I
say to them?"

And God said to Moses, "I AM WHO I
AM." And He said, "Thus you shall say to the
children of Israel, 'I AM has sent me to you.'"

Exodus 3:13–14

For with God nothing will be impossible.

Luke 1:37

Great is the LORD, and greatly to be praised;
And His greatness is unsearchable.
One generation shall praise Your works
      to another,
And shall declare Your mighty acts.
Your kingdom is an everlasting kingdom,
And Your dominion endures throughout
      all generations.

Psalm 145:3–4, 13

Whom have I in heaven but You?
And there is none upon earth that I
desire besides You.

Psalm 73:25

For thus says the High and Lofty One
Who inhabits eternity, whose name is Holy:
"I dwell in the high and holy place,
With him who has a contrite and
humble spirit,
To revive the spirit of the humble,
And to revive the heart of the contrite ones."

Isaiah 57:15

The heavens declare the glory of God;
And the firmament shows His handiwork.

Psalm 19:1

Behold, I am the LORD, the God of all flesh.
Is there anything too hard for Me?

Jeremiah 32:27

In the beginning God created the heavens
and the earth. The earth was without form, and
void; and darkness was on the face of the deep.
And the Spirit of God was hovering over the face
of the waters. Then God said, "Let there be light";
and there was light.

Genesis 1:1–3

"Am I a God near at hand," says the LORD,
"And not a God afar off?
Can anyone hide himself in secret places,
So I shall not see him?" says the LORD;
"Do I not fill heaven and earth?" says
the LORD.

Jeremiah 23:23–24

For of Him and through Him and to Him
are all things, to whom be glory forever.

Romans 11:36

Hope for Revival

For your light has come!
And the glory of the LORD is risen upon you.
For behold, the darkness shall cover
    the earth,
And deep darkness the people;
But the LORD will arise over you,
And His glory will be seen upon you.

Isaiah 60:1–2

All the ends of the world
Shall remember and turn to the LORD,
And all the families of the nations
Shall worship before You.
For the kingdom is the LORD's,
And He rules over the nations.

Psalm 22:27–28

For the earth will be filled
With the knowledge of the glory of the LORD,
As the waters cover the sea.

Habakkuk 2:14

This gospel of the kingdom will be preached
in all the world as a witness to all the nations, and
then the end will come.

Matthew 24:14

The voice of one crying in the wilderness:
"Prepare the way of the LORD;
Make straight in the desert
A highway for our God.
Every valley shall be exalted
And every mountain and hill brought low;
The crooked places shall be made straight
And the rough places smooth;
The glory of the LORD shall be revealed,
And all flesh shall see it together;
For the mouth of the LORD has spoken."

Isaiah 40:3–5

The LORD has made bare His holy arm
In the eyes of all the nations;
And all the ends of the earth shall see
The salvation of our God.
So shall He sprinkle many nations.
Kings shall shut their mouths at Him;
For what had not been told them they
        shall see,
And what they had not heard they shall
        consider.

Isaiah 52:10, 15

I will seek what was lost and bring back
what was driven away, bind up the broken and
strengthen what was sick; but I will destroy the fat
and the strong, and feed them in judgment.

Ezekiel 34:16

Indeed the LORD has proclaimed
To the end of the world:
"Say to the daughter of Zion,
'Surely your salvation is coming;
Behold, His reward is with Him,
And His work before Him.'"
And they shall call them The Holy People,
The Redeemed of the LORD;
And you shall be called Sought Out,
A City Not Forsaken.

Isaiah 62:11–12

I will show wonders in the heavens and in
      the earth:
Blood and fire and pillars of smoke.
The sun shall be turned into darkness,
And the moon into blood,
Before the coming of the great and awesome
      day of the LORD.
And it shall come to pass
That whoever calls on the name of the LORD
Shall be saved.
For in Mount Zion and in Jerusalem
      there shall be deliverance,
As the LORD has said,
Among the remnant whom the LORD calls.

Joel 2:30–32

Search for Signs of Eternity

Heaven and earth will pass away, but My words will by no means pass away.

Matthew 24:35

The Spirit expressly says that in latter times some will depart from the faith, giving heed to deceiving spirits and doctrines of demons, speaking lies in hypocrisy, having their own conscience seared with a hot iron, forbidding to marry, and commanding to abstain from foods which God created to be received with thanksgiving by those who believe and know the truth.

1 Timothy 4:1–3

Know this, that in the last days perilous times will come: For men will be lovers of themselves, lovers of money, boasters, proud, blasphemers, disobedient to parents, unthankful, unholy, unloving, unforgiving, slanderers, without self-control, brutal, despisers of good, traitors, headstrong, haughty, lovers of pleasure rather than lovers of God, having a form of godliness but denying its power. And from such people turn away!

2 Timothy 3:1–5

For since the beginning of the world
Men have not heard nor perceived by the ear,
Nor has the eye seen any God besides You,
Who acts for the one who waits for Him.

Isaiah 64:4

For the wages of sin is death, but the gift of God is eternal life in Christ Jesus our Lord.

Romans 6:23

Jesus answered and said to them: "Take heed that no one deceives you. For many will come in My name, saying, 'I am the Christ,' and will deceive many. And you will hear of wars and rumors of wars. See that you are not troubled; for all these things must come to pass, but the end is not yet. For nation will rise against nation, and kingdom against kingdom. And there will be famines, pestilences, and earthquakes in various places.

All these are the beginning of sorrows. Then they will deliver you up to tribulation and kill you, and you will be hated by all nations for My name's sake. And then many will be offended, will betray one another, and will hate one another. Then many false prophets will rise up and deceive many. And because lawlessness will abound, the love of many will grow cold. But he who endures to the end shall be saved. And this gospel of the kingdom will be preached in all the world as a witness to all the nations, and then the end will come."

Matthew 24:4–14

Then two men will be in the field: one will be taken and the other left.

Watch therefore, for you do not know what hour your Lord is coming.

Therefore you also be ready, for the Son of Man is coming at an hour you do not expect.

Matthew 24:40, 42, 44

And it shall come to pass in the last days,
    says God,
That I will pour out of My Spirit on all flesh;
Your sons and your daughters shall prophesy,
Your young men shall see visions,
Your old men shall dream dreams.
And on My menservants and on My
    maidservants
I will pour out My Spirit in those days;
And they shall prophesy.
I will show wonders in heaven above
And signs in the earth beneath:
Blood and fire and vapor of smoke.
The sun shall be turned into darkness,
And the moon into blood,
Before the coming of the great and
    awesome day of the LORD.
And it shall come to pass
That whoever calls on the name of the LORD
Shall be saved.

Acts 2:17–21

There are also celestial bodies and terrestrial bodies; but the glory of the celestial is one, and the glory of the terrestrial is another.

So also is the resurrection of the dead. The body is sown in corruption, it is raised in incorruption. It is sown in dishonor, it is raised in glory. It is sown in weakness, it is raised in power. It is sown a natural body, it is raised a spiritual body. There is a natural body, and there is a spiritual body.

1 Corinthians 15:40, 42–44

Behold, I tell you a mystery: We shall not all sleep, but we shall all be changed—in a moment, in the twinkling of an eye, at the last trumpet. For the trumpet will sound, and the dead will be raised incorruptible, and we shall be changed. For this corruptible must put on incorruption, and this mortal must put on immortality. So when this corruptible has put on incorruption, and this mortal has put on immortality, then shall be brought to pass the saying that is written: Death is swallowed up in victory.

O Death, where is your sting?
O Hades, where is your victory?
The sting of death is sin, and the strength of sin is the law. But thanks be to God, who gives us the victory through our Lord Jesus Christ.

1 Corinthians 15:51–57

Beloved, now we are children of God; and it has not yet been revealed what we shall be, but we know that when He is revealed, we shall be like Him, for we shall see Him as He is. And everyone who has this hope in Him purifies himself, just as He is pure.

1 John 3:2–3

I do not want you to be ignorant, brethren, concerning those who have fallen asleep, lest you sorrow as others who have no hope. For if we believe that Jesus died and rose again, even so God will bring with Him those who sleep in Jesus.

For this we say to you by the word of the Lord, that we who are alive and remain until the coming of the Lord will by no means precede those who are asleep. For the Lord Himself will descend from heaven with a shout, with the voice of an archangel, and with the trumpet of God. And the dead in Christ will rise first. Then we who are alive and remain shall be caught up together with them in the clouds to meet the Lord in the air. And thus we shall always be with the Lord. Therefore comfort one another with these words.

1 Thessalonians 4:13–18

Dynamic Women of
Faith . . .

Mary—Mother of Jesus

Now in the sixth month the angel Gabriel was sent by God to a city of Galilee named Nazareth, to a virgin betrothed to a man whose name was Joseph, of the house of David. The virgin's name was Mary. And having come in, the angel said to her, "Rejoice, highly favored one, the Lord is with you; blessed are you among women!"

But when she saw him, she was troubled at his saying, and considered what manner of greeting this was. Then the angel said to her, "Do not be afraid, Mary, for you have found favor with God. And behold, you will conceive in your womb and bring forth a Son, and shall call His name JESUS."

Luke 1:26–31

Now there stood by the cross of Jesus His mother, and His mother's sister, Mary the wife of Clopas, and Mary Magdalene. When Jesus therefore saw His mother, and the disciple whom He loved standing by, He said to His mother, "Woman, behold your son!" Then He said to the disciple, "Behold your mother!" And from that hour that disciple took her to his own home.

John 19:25–27

And Mary said:
"My soul magnifies the Lord,
And my spirit has rejoiced in God my Savior.
For He has regarded the lowly state of
     His maidservant;
For behold, henceforth all generations
     will call me blessed.
For He who is mighty has done great
     things for me,
And holy is His name.
And His mercy is on those who fear Him
From generation to generation.
He has shown strength with His arm;
He has scattered the proud in the
     imagination of their hearts.
He has put down the mighty from
     their thrones,
And exalted the lowly.
He has filled the hungry with good things,
And the rich He has sent away empty."

Luke 1:46–53

Elizabeth—Mother of John the Baptist 🌿

There was in the days of Herod, the king of Judea, a certain priest named Zacharias, of the division of Abijah. His wife was of the daughters of Aaron, and her name was Elizabeth. And they were both righteous before God, walking in all the commandments and ordinances of the Lord blameless. But they had no child, because Elizabeth was barren, and they were both well advanced in years.

Luke 1:5–7

The angel said to him, "Do not be afraid, Zacharias, for your prayer is heard; and your wife Elizabeth will bear you a son, and you shall call his name John."

Luke 1:13

Now indeed, Elizabeth your relative has also conceived a son in her old age; and this is now the sixth month for her who was called barren. For with God nothing will be impossible.

Luke 1:36–37

You, child, will be called the prophet of
  the Highest;
For you will go before the face of the Lord
  to prepare His ways,
To give knowledge of salvation to His people
By the remission of their sins.

Luke 1:76–77

It happened, when Elizabeth heard the greeting of Mary, that the babe leaped in her womb; and Elizabeth was filled with the Holy Spirit. Then she spoke out with a loud voice and said, "Blessed are you among women, and blessed is the fruit of your womb! But why is this granted to me, that the mother of my Lord should come to me? For indeed, as soon as the voice of your greeting sounded in my ears, the babe leaped in my womb for joy. Blessed is she who believed, for there will be a fulfillment of those things which were told her from the Lord."

Luke 1:41–45

Sarah—Wife of Abraham

Then God said to Abraham, "As for Sarai your wife, you shall not call her name Sarai, but Sarah shall be her name. And I will bless her and also give you a son by her; then I will bless her, and she shall be a mother of nations; kings of peoples shall be from her."

Genesis 17:15–16

Then God said: "No, Sarah your wife shall bear you a son, and you shall call his name Isaac; I will establish My covenant with him for an everlasting covenant, and with his descendants after him."

Genesis 17:19

The LORD visited Sarah as He had said, and the LORD did for Sarah as He had spoken. For Sarah conceived and bore Abraham a son in his old age, at the set time of which God had spoken to him. And Abraham called the name of his son who was born to him—whom Sarah bore to him—Isaac.

Genesis 21:1–3

God said to Abraham, "Do not let it be displeasing in your sight because of the lad or because of your bondwoman. Whatever Sarah has said to you, listen to her voice; for in Isaac your seed shall be called."

Genesis 21:12

By faith Sarah herself also received strength to conceive seed, and she bore a child when she was was past the age, because she judged Him faithful who had promised.

Hebrews 11:11

Hannah—Mother of Samuel 🌿

She was in bitterness of soul, and prayed to the LORD and wept in anguish. Then she made a vow and said, "O LORD of hosts, if You will indeed look on the affliction of Your maidservant and remember me, and not forget Your maidservant, but will give Your maidservant a male child, then I will give him to the LORD all the days of his life, and no razor shall come upon his head."

1 Samuel 1:10–11

It came to pass in the process of time that Hannah conceived and bore a son, and called his name Samuel, saying, "Because I have asked for him from the LORD."

1 Samuel 1:20

The LORD has granted me my petition which I asked of Him. Therefore I also have lent him to the LORD; as long as he lives he shall be lent to the LORD. So they worshiped the LORD there.

1 Samuel 1:27–28

The LORD visited Hannah, so that she conceived and bore three sons and two daughters. Meanwhile the child Samuel grew before the LORD.

1 Samuel 2:21

Ruth—Great Grandmother of David 🌼

Boaz answered and said to her, "It has been fully reported to me, all that you have done for your mother-in-law since the death of your husband, and how you have left your father and your mother and the land of your birth, and have come to a people whom you did not know before. The LORD repay your work, and a full reward be given you by the LORD God of Israel, under whose wings you have come for refuge."

Then she said, "Let me find favor in your sight, my lord; for you have comforted me, and have spoken kindly to your maidservant, though I am not like one of your maidservants."

Ruth 2:11–13

Blessed are you of the LORD, my daughter! For you have shown more kindness at the end than at the beginning, in that you did not go after young men, whether poor or rich. And now, my daughter, do not fear. I will do for you all that you request, for all the people of my town know that you are a virtuous woman.

Ruth 3:10–11

So Boaz took Ruth and she became his wife; and when he went in to her, the LORD gave her conception, and she bore a son.

Ruth 4:13

The neighbor women gave him a name, saying, "There is a son born to Naomi." And they called his name Obed. He is the father of Jesse, the father of David.

Ruth 4:17

Lydia—Seller of Purple (Merchant) 🌸

On the Sabbath day we went out of the city to the riverside, where prayer was customarily made; and we sat down and spoke to the women who met there. Now a certain woman named Lydia heard us. She was a seller of purple from the city of Thyatira, who worshiped God. The Lord opened her heart to heed the things spoken by Paul. And when she and her household were baptized, she begged us, saying, "If you have judged me to be faithful to the Lord, come to my house and stay." So she persuaded us.

Acts 16:13–15

When it was day, the magistrates sent the officers, saying, "Let those men go."

So they went out of the prison and entered the house of Lydia; and when they had seen the brethren, they encouraged them and departed.

Acts 16:35, 40

VERSES THAT ARE SPECIAL TO ME

_____

_____
_____
_____
_____
_____
_____
_____
_____
_____
_____
_____
_____
_____
_____
_____
_____
_____
_____
_____
_____
_____
_____

VERSES THAT ARE SPECIAL TO ME

_____

_____

_____

_____

_____

_____

_____

_____

_____

_____

_____

_____

_____

_____

_____

_____

_____

_____

_____

_____

_____

_____

PRAYERS FOR MY LOVED ONES

_____

_____

_____

_____

_____

_____

_____

_____

_____

_____

_____

_____

_____

_____

_____

_____

_____

_____

_____

_____

ANSWERED PRAYERS

PRAYER REQUESTS

_____

_____

_____

_____

_____

_____

_____

_____

_____

_____

_____

_____

_____

_____

_____

_____

_____

_____

_____

_____

_____

_____

_____

ANSWERED PRAYERS

_____

_____

_____

_____

_____

_____

_____

_____

_____

_____

_____

_____

_____

_____

_____

_____

_____

_____

_____

_____

_____

_____

NOTES

NOTES

NOTES